D&S
VOL. 47

SAC's "LONG RIFLE"
OF THE 1950'S

B-36
PEACEMAKER

in detail & scale

Wayne Wachsmuth

squadron/signal publications

COPYRIGHT © 1997 BY DETAIL & SCALE, INC.

This book is a product of Detail & Scale, Inc., which has sole responsibility for its content and layout, except that all contributors are responsible for the security clearance and copyright release of all materials submitted. Published by Squadron/Signal Publications, 1115 Crowley Drive, Carrollton, Texas 75011. ISBN 1-888974-05-2

CONTRIBUTORS AND SOURCES:

Dave Anderton
H. Applegate
COL Knox Bishop, USAF (Ret)
J. C. Campbell
Roger Cripliver
George Cully
Jim Galloway
MAJ John Hardison, USAF
Tom Hitchcock
Geoff Hayes

Marty Isham
Lloyd Jones
Bert Kinzey
Alwyn Lloyd
Dave Menard
Jim Mesko
Mike Moore
C. Nelson
E. S. Quandt
William Steeneck

Kathy Wachsmuth
R. E. Williams
Mark Young
American Aviation Historical Society
General Dynamics/Lockheed, Fort Worth
National Archives
United States Air Force
United States Air Force Museum
United States Air Force Historical Research Center

Special thanks are due to Mike Moore, who so untiringly mined the files at General Dynamics/Lockheed, Fort Worth.

Many photographs in this publication are credited to their contributors. Photographs with no credit indicated were taken by the author.

Wachsmuth, Wayne, 1935–
    B-36 Peacemaker: in detail & scale/Wayne Wachsmuth.
    p. cm. -- (D & S ; vol. 47)
    "A Detail & Scale aviation publication."—Verso.
    "SAC's 'long rifle' of the 1950's—Verso.
    Includes bibliographical references.
    ISBN 0-89024-239-9

Front cover: Two B-36H aircraft, 51-5726 and 52-1358, were operated by the 4925th Test Group (Atomic) for weapons test drops in the 1950s. The paint scheme was identical on both sides of each aircraft with two exceptions on the vertical tail. On 52-1358, the tail number (which was 21358) had a bare metal background instead of being painted directly on the white as seen here. Second, on 52-1358, the vertical fin and rudder were left unpainted above the top rudder hinge. The colors appear to be insignia red, white, and blue. The wings and center section of the fuselage are natural metal.

(USAF via Cully)

Rear cover, top: The pilots' instrument panels on the flight deck of a B-36J belie the size of the aircraft with just the flight instruments, warning lights, indicators for flaps and trim tabs, and the jet engine instruments.

Rear cover, bottom: The really busy panel is the one manned by the two flight engineers. It contains all of the performance and analyzing instruments for the six R-4360 reciprocating engines as well as for the hydraulic and electrical systems.

INTRODUCTION

The XB-36 sits near the edge of the ramp at Fort Worth. Note that the original single main wheel units have been replaced by the later four-wheel design. The cleanliness of the airframe is readily apparent from this angle. (USAF)

The initial requirement for a heavy bomber with intercontinental range dates back to 1941 when there was uncertainty as to whether England would eventually fall under the military might of Nazi Germany. Without bases in England to operate from, any involvement in the war by the United States would require a bomber with trans-Atlantic range. But England survived, and the success of the island hopping campaign in the Pacific meant that the B-17s, B-24s, and B-29s were adequate to meet the strategic bombing requirements of World War II. But as the world entered the nuclear age, the necessity for an intercontinental bomber was renewed, and the program that would eventually lead to the production of the B-36 Peacemaker was continued.

In the early 1940s, before the introduction of high-tech designs, high speeds, and fuel efficient engines, any aircraft with intercontinental range would of necessity be very large, if for no other reason than to accommodate the enormous amount of fuel required for the trip. The B-36 was indeed a giant aircraft. It was so big that, in addition to the name, "Peacemaker," it was also often referred to as "The Aluminum Cloud." Years after its retirement, it still remains the largest combat aircraft ever built. With advances in all areas of aerodynamics, propulsion, and weapons systems, it is probable that the B-36 will forever retain this distinction in the annals of aviation history. The Peacemaker should also be remembered as the first bomber designed primarily to deter war rather than to wage it.

Very little has been written about the B-36, and what is available does not get into much detail about this unique aircraft. Very few photographs of its many unusual features have been published. In 1990, former SAC bomber pilot and modeler, Wayne Wachsmuth, decided to do a book on the B-36 in the Detail & Scale Series. Wayne spent four years traveling, taking photographs, and doing research. His trips took him to Maxwell AFB,

Chanute AFB, and Wright Patterson AFB on three different occasions. Research was also conducted at the National Archives and at the National Air and Space Museum.

Wayne begins this book with a look at the development of the B-36 from its first inception in 1941 to its operation with the U. S. Air Force. But the primary focus of this publication, as it is with all of the books in the Detail & Scale Series, is on the many physical details of the aircraft. Included are close-up photographs and drawings of everything from the cockpits to the bomb bays, and from the landing gear to the defensive armament systems. Also illustrated are both the reciprocating and jet engines, antenna installations, lighting systems, and the ECM gear used on the huge bomber. Photographs and information about test aircraft, the FICON version, and RB-36s are also included. Wayne has also done the five-view scale drawings specifically for this publication rather than rely on previously released drawings. All of these features combine to make this the most detailed look at the B-36 Peacemaker ever published.

Our usual Modelers Section is also included, and Wayne has covered the Monogram 1/72nd scale B-36 in extensive detail with respect to corrections, modifications, and conversions. Decals available for this kit are also covered along with brief reviews of the older scale models of this famous bomber.

Wayne received a lot of assistance during the time he worked on this book, and a list of contributors can be found on page 2. A special thanks goes to Mike Moore of General Dynamics/Lockheed who time and again went through company files to locate unique and unusual photographs that simply could not be found anywhere else. Some of these photographs were "rescued" as they were on the way out of the building to be destroyed. To Mike and all of the contributors, Wayne and Detail & Scale express a sincere word of thanks for helping make this book possible.

DEVELOPMENTAL HISTORY

The original request for a "long range bomber" was issued in 1941 when it was feared that England would fall to the German military. This request would eventually result in the B-36 which became SAC's first intercontinental bomber during the 1950s.

(USAF)

Fearing the collapse of England under the weight of the German military, the U. S. Army Air Corps (USAAC) released a request for proposals (RFP) in April 1941 calling for the development of a long range bomber that could attack targets in Europe from bases in the United States. Among the initial requirements for the bomber were a top speed of 450 miles per hour at 25,000 feet, a cruising speed of 275 miles per hour, and a service ceiling of 45,000 feet. Most important was the range requirement of 12,000 miles at an altitude of 25,000 feet. To put these requirements in perspective, the B-17E had a top speed of 317 miles per hour at 25,000 feet, a service ceiling of 37,000 feet, and a range of 2,000 miles. So the new bomber was to have a range which was six times that of the existing B-17.

It became clear that these requirements were too demanding if rapid development was to be a prime concern, and by August 1941, the specifications were revised downward to a cruising speed between 240 and 300 miles per hour, a service ceiling of 40,000 feet, and an overall range of 10,000 miles. Most significant was the requirement for a combat radius of 4,000 miles with a 10,000 pound bomb load.

The tidal wave of Nazi military successes broke up on the rock of RAF resistance, thus removing the initial reason for the development of an intercontinental bomber. However, the program found numerous opportunities to

cling to life through the next eighteen years.

Preliminary proposals were submitted by Boeing, Consolidated, and Douglas, and by early October, the Materiel Division of the U. S. Army Air Force (USAAF formally replaced the USAAC on 20 June, 1941) suggested action on the Consolidated proposal. This led to a contract approval on 15 November, 1941, which called for production of two prototypes of the experimental long range bomber which was designated Model 35 by Consolidated. Proposals had been submitted for designs with four and six engines, and a week after the contract approval, the Wright Field Engineering Division completed its analysis and opted for the configuration with six engines.

The initial work on the project was started at Consolidated's San Diego plant with much of the effort being spent in refining the design to reduce weight and drag. At the same time, a full scale wooden mockup of what had become known as the XB-36 was constructed to check the configuration and equipment fit. In the interim, Consolidated also changed its designation from Model 35 to Model 36 in order to avoid confusion.

In July 1942, the Army Air Force sent a team to San Diego to inspect the finished mockup. During the inspection the team split into two factions. Some of the members wanted to reduce the defensive armament and crew in order to decrease the weight so that the 10,000-mile range requirement could be met. Others argued that

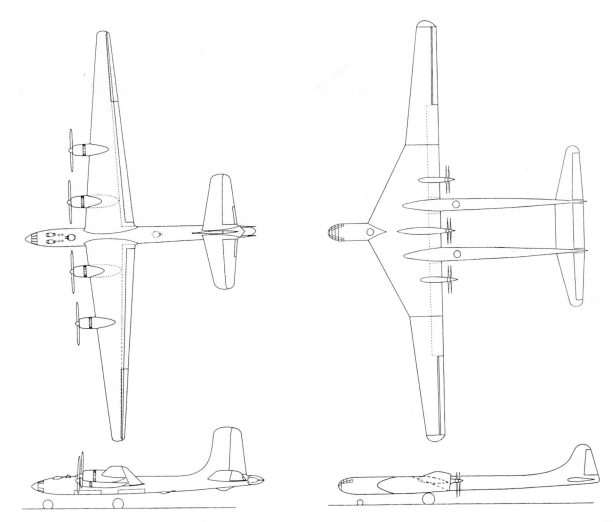

At left is a drawing of the Douglas response to the RFP for an intercontinental bomber. It shows features that would appear in later designs. The Boeing entry, shown at right, was nothing if not huge. It had a wingspan of 270 feet!

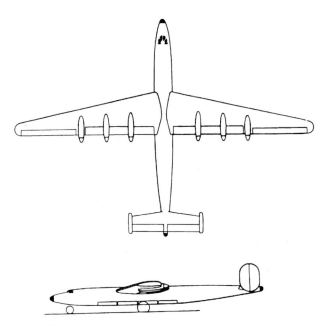

The original six-engine design submitted by Consolidated had a wing plan form that would remain constant throughout the life of the program.

a 10,000-mile range was of little consequence if the bomber could not defend itself over the target. As a result, a compromise was reached whereby "less necessary" equipment would be deleted to the point where the range figure could be maintained. This allowed the program to be continued for the time being.

Within a month of the mockup inspection, Consolidated recommended shifting the program from its San Diego plant to the new government-leased facility in Fort Worth, Texas. The move was accomplished in less than a month, and it started a long association with the Fort Worth area that lasted until 1993 when Lockheed bought that part of what had since become Convair and then General Dynamics. The move, although expeditiously accomplished, did cause a several month delay in the schedule, and Consolidated proposed to the Army Air Force that time could be gained by starting preliminary production work on a concurrent basis with the construction of the prototypes and the initial flight testing.

According to the company, as much as two years could be cut from the time it would take to get the bomber operational if development and production work proceeded simultaneously. Facing military setbacks and more immediate problems on the war front, the AAF felt the diversion of already scarce resources was not justified,

The Consolidated mock-up was very similar to the initial drawings. This picture, dated July 1942, was taken at the San Diego plant. Less that two months later, the project was shifted to the new plant at Fort Worth, Texas.

(National Archives)

so they did not follow up on Consolidated's offer. At the same time, the company requested funds to develop a cargo version (XC-99) believing that without the systems required by the bomber, the airframe could be ready for engine, gear, and flight characteristic testing much earlier. The AAF approved the project, but they inserted the proviso that one of the two bombers would be produced

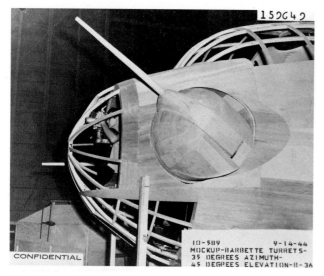

Experience in Europe had demonstrated the need for forward firing guns, and this September 1944 photograph shows one of the proposed configurations.

(National Archives)

at least three months before the cargo aircraft.

As the war continued on into 1943, it appeared that a weapon would be needed to strike Japan from long distances, especially since it seemed that China with its potential for bases would be lost. None of the bombers then operational could span the huge reaches of the Pacific, and the B-29 project was mired in developmental problems. With that in mind, General Arnold directed in June 1943 that 100 B-36 aircraft be purchased as long as no major problems in production were discovered.

Due to the availability problems with testing facilities and slow progress with the Pratt & Whitney Wasp engine, little progress was made through the rest of 1943 or the first half of 1944. By then, the changing war situation threw yet another wrench into the works. By that time, the American advance in the Pacific had reached the Marianas, and bases on these islands were within B-29 range of Japan. Production difficulties with the B-29 were also nearing solutions, and the AAF wanted the B-32 project pushed as a possible backup. These factors resulted in the B-36 being moved to the far back burner for the time being. The formal contract specified delivery of the first B-36 in August 1946, with number 100 due that October. How realistic this schedule was would be apparent in the coming months.

In mid-1945, victory in the Pacific war was near, and contracts were cut back if not cancelled entirely. But the B-36 dodged another bullet when the butcher's bill for capturing advanced bases in the Pacific was totaled. It was obvious that a bomber that did not need those bases

The initial configuration of the XB-36 included single large main landing gear wheels. With the exception of the change to the single vertical stabilizer and rudder combination, it greatly resembles the original drawings. **(USAF)**

would save lives in future conflicts. A second and perhaps larger consideration was the knowledge that an American monopoly on the atomic bomb would not last forever, and retaliation in case of nuclear attack could not wait for far flung bases to be captured. With these considerations in mind, the Air Staff recommended continuation of the B-36 project in August 1945.

While all of the pulling and shoving about the future of the airplane was going on, the development had been continuing, and there were plenty of problems to solve. The first major change had been made in October 1943, when the original twin tail configuration was switched to a single fin design. This saved nearly 4,000 pounds, increased stability, and reduced drag.

European experience had demonstrated the need for nose armament, so the entire nose section and cockpit was redesigned in late 1944 in order to add defensive armament and raise the canopy for better visibility. This change, combined with additional radio and radar equipment, added back most of the weight that had been saved with the redesign of the tail. Meanwhile, the weight of the engines also continued to grow, adding yet another ton to the design weight of the aircraft. Magnesium was used as extensively as possible to try to keep the weight from growing out of control.

Much attention had also been given to reducing drag on the airframe, and what had been chin type intakes mounted on the lower surface of the wings were changed to the now familiar leading edge intakes. These provided both cooling and engine carburetion air. The retractable gun turrets were also an attempt to reduce drag.

The final configuration of the aircraft was conventional with the exception of mounting the engines on the trailing edges of the wings so that they acted as pushers. This allowed for a large reduction in the frontal area normally associated with radial engines.

In spite of all the attempts to keep the weight down, the aircraft was so heavy that if the original main landing gear with its single large wheel design was retained, there would be only three runways in the United States capable of supporting the new bomber! This caused much effort to be spent on alternatives including a design with treads. But when advances in brake technology allowed the use of smaller diameter wheels, a system with four wheels for each main gear strut was developed. This permitted the B-36 to operate from any runway capable of supporting the B-29.

As 1945 ended, there were still difficulties with the program, not the least of which were labor and workmanship troubles at the Fort Worth plant of what was now known as the Convair Aircraft Company. Additionally, some high ranking officers predicted grave structural limitations and failure of the project. So it came as great relief when the prototype lifted off the runway on 8 August, 1946, for the first time. The maiden flight lasted thirty-seven minutes, and even though it was not exactly trouble free, this significant milestone was finally passed.

Flight testing proceeded in earnest, and by the following August much had been learned. A more powerful version of the Pratt & Whitney Wasp Major, adding 500 horsepower per engine, would be installed in the B-36B aircraft. This improvement increased both

Above: A cockpit photograph in the XB-36 shows Convair test pilots B. A. Erickson (L) and Gus Green (R) at a very simple panel with excellent forward and side visibility. The top of the flight engineer's seat can be seen at the lower right, and it is facing outboard. (USAF)

Left: This is the flight engineer's panel in the XB-36. As full as it was, this station would grow in complexity until the B-36H and J variants required two flight engineers to properly monitor and control all of the aircraft's many complex systems. (USAF)

This in-flight shot of the XB-36 shows the main gear with its large single wheels to good advantage. Also visible is the extended tail bumper that was a feature on B-36A and B variants. *(USAF)*

In order to reduce the footprint pressure of the large single wheels, the XB-36 was equipped with a tread type main gear as seen here. This photograph was taken as the aircraft lifted off from the runway at Fort Worth for a test flight. Note also that the nose gear has a tread design as well. Detailed photographs of this unusual landing gear can be found on page 49. *(USAF)*

This in-flight photograph of the XB-36 shows the lack of a bulge on the top inner wing panel that would be needed later when the four-wheel main gear was installed. *(USAF)*

speed and service ceiling. An even more powerful engine, fitted with a variable discharge turbine (VDT), was to be installed in the last thirty-four aircraft out of the production run that totaled one hundred, and these were to be designated B-36Cs. However, problems with this engine and the supercharger proved insurmountable, so these aircraft were completed as B-36Bs.

Along the way, the development of a new main landing gear reduced weight distribution and opened a large number of airfields for use by the B-36 fleet. More aircraft were just starting to emerge from the Fort Worth plant to enter testing in late 1947. The YB-36 took to the air in December, and evaluation began in earnest. (The B-36A that flew in August of that year had only minimum equipment required for flight and went to Wright-Patterson Air Force Base for static testing.) Factory testing took longer than usual, and it was not until May 1949 that the Air Force (having become a separate service in 1947) accepted the YB-36 and began its own evaluations on that particular airframe. (By that time the YB-36 had been brought up to B-36A standards, and it joined other B-36As in the test and evaluation program.)

Yet another program review had been completed in 1948 when the VDT engine project came apart. The two components (engine and turbine) worked well on their own, but proved to have unsolvable cooling problems when combined. This resulted in the cancellation of the B-36C variant as mentioned above. But comparisons with the other piston engined bomber available at that time (B-

50) still gave a slight edge to the B-36, which was proving to be better than anticipated during testing.

The Soviets also gave an unintended boost to the B-36 when they blockaded West Berlin in 1948. By June of that year, the 7th Bomb Group (redesignated the 7th Bomb Wing in 1951) at Carswell AFB received the first of twenty-two B-36As they would use for training and familiarization. None of these B-36As were equipped with defensive armament, and because necessary dimensions were withheld from the manufacturer for security reasons, none of the existing nuclear weapons would fit in the bomb bays!

The problems with the B-36A were pushed into the background by the delivery of B-36B models to the 7th Bomb Group in November 1948, and no time was lost assessing its performance. On 7-8 December (coincidental timing?) a B-36B flew from Carswell AFB to Hawaii and dropped a dummy 10,000-pound bomb. It then returned to its home base without refueling. The distance covered was over 8,000 miles, and the fact that the raid was not detected by the defenses in Hawaii caused red faces all around.

The B-36B was a large step up from the earlier B-36A, and improvements included the more powerful R-4360-41 engine, the newer AN/APQ-24 bombing-navigation radar set, and the defensive armament of sixteen 20-mm cannons. These cannon were located in the nose and tail turrets and under sliding doors on the top and bottom of the fuselage. The bomb bay had also undergone modifica-

The YB-36 was built to the production configuration. The most obvious change from the XB-36 was in the cockpit area. Also note that the large single-wheel design is still being used for the main landing gear. **(General Dynamics)**

tions so that it could carry existing nuclear weapons, and eighteen B-36Bs were equipped to carry and guide the remote controlled "Tarzon" bomb.

In early 1949, yet another threat to the program's existence was weathered when, in the course of service rivalry with the Navy, a document (anonymously authored) circulated in Washington charging corruption and in-competence in the contracting and the inability of the aircraft to perform its mission. An investigation by the House Armed Services Sub-committee found there was no substance to the charges, largely by tracking down the author and putting him under oath. While the bickering between the services as to which of them should be the primary global deterrent force continued, a new develop-

The first B-36A off of the production line was flown to Wright-Patterson AFB for structural test. It lacked much of the operational equipment found in the production models. However, this aircraft is fitted with the four-wheel main landing gear. **(USAF)**

The XB, YB, and the B-36A and B variants were equipped with sliding bomb bay doors seen here in the partly open position. Doors on bays 1 and 4 slid up the left side of the fuselage, while those on bays 2 and 3 were split on the centerline and slid up each side. This was due to the limited space under the wings　　　　*(USAF)*

ment increased the capabilities of the Peacemaker.

The addition of jet engines to the aircraft had been proposed by Convair in October 1948, but lack of funding delayed a "go-ahead" on the project until January 1949. By late March, a prototype using Allison J35-A-19 engines on B-36B, 44-92057, was airborne, and it confirmed the benefits of the modification. By June, the definitive configuration was under test, and it used General Electric J47-GE-19 engines in a pod that was nearly identical to that used for the inboard engines on the B-47. While it would be a year before the first B-36D was handed over to the Air Force, the upgrade affected the existing fleet.

The B-36D retained the same piston engines as the previous versions, but the four jet engines were added. It also had the more capable K-3A bombing and navigation radar and the newer AN/APG-32 tail gun radar. At the same time, the sliding bomb bay doors were replaced with "snap action" doors that could open or close in two seconds. While approval of the modifications came too late for most of the B-36Bs that were still on the production line, the last eleven Bs were modified to B-36D standards before being accepted by the Air Force.

Only twenty-two B-36D and sixteen RB-36D airframes were built as such from the start, with the remainder being updated to D standards at Convair's San Diego plant. This led to some confusion as to the total numbers of each type that were produced. Of the eighty-six B-36D aircraft that were built, sixty-four started life as B-36Bs and were referred to as such by Convair. Additionally, of the twenty-four RB-36Ds produced, only sixteen were manufactured as such from the start, and the remaining six were converted from B-36Bs.

In early 1950, the remaining twenty-two B-36As were upgraded to the RB-36E configuration. This included adding the 4360-41 engines, the jet pods, and converting sixteen feet of the forward bomb bay to a camera compartment manned by photo-recce crewmen. Additionally, electronic surveillance equipment and operators were added, and this increased the number in the crew to twenty-two, seven more than for a B-36D bomber.

As the B-36 fleet continued to grow in number, General Curtis LeMay became the new commander of what by then had become known as the Strategic Air Command (SAC). General LeMay instituted policies that would give the organization a reputation for professionalism that it would carry until it was disbanded in 1992. Intensive training and constant evaluation were combined with a refusal to accept anything less than maximum performance. This molded SAC into a finely tuned instrument capable of striking targets anywhere in the world on short notice. However, all was not rosy, as there were the inevitable developmental problems with the Peacemaker to overcome.

Deficiencies with the electrical system, problems with the defensive armament, and fuel leaks plagued the aircraft and continued with the arrival of the B-36F in 1951. The B-36F was powered by R 4360-53 engines rated at an extra 300 horsepower each over the -41 version, and this improved performance. The new version was also equipped with the K-3A bombing system and the AN/APG-32A gunnery radar which incorporated twin radomes for aiming the tail gun.

While the B-36F and RB-36F aircraft entered service, work was already progressing on the B-36H. (The YB-36G designation was given to the aircraft that was later redesignated YB-60. This all-jet version of the Peacemaker was designed to compete with the B-52.) The first B-36H was delivered to the Air Force in December 1951, and with this new variant, SAC finally had what looked like a mature weapons system with the earlier problems now under control. Major differences included a revised flight deck with seating provided for a second flight engineer and an upgraded AN/APG-41A gun laying radar for the tail turret.

In 1952, two further problems surfaced causing a flurry of activity until fixes were completed. Altitude restrictions were placed on the fleet after a bulkhead on an RB-36 blew out at 33,000 feet. Once the fleet was inspected for faulty bulkheads and the bad ones replaced, this restriction was removed. The entire fleet of later model aircraft was grounded for a time after several ground accidents indicated a problem with the main gear pivot shaft. This restriction was short lived, because the fix was easily accomplished.

The B-36J was the last model to enter service, and it became operational in September 1953. The J had only minor changes over the B-36H, and these included a stronger landing gear and additional fuel tanks. By this time, the design of the B-36 had reached maturity, and its eventual replacement, the B-52, had flown in April 1952. This caused further development of the Peacemaker to be cancelled. The final B-36J was delivered to the Air Force on 10 August, 1954, some thirteen years after the original request for proposal was submitted.

In 1954, all of SAC's RB-36 wings had their primary mission changed to bombing instead of reconnaissance, and this caused major airframe changes. The aft ECM equipment bay was moved from bomb bay 4 to the area aft of the rear crew compartment, and the three bomb bays were converted to carry special weapons. This meant strengthening bulkheads, replacing external panels, and installing new bomb bay doors. By October 1955, all of the heavy strategic reconnaissance wings were converted and redesignated heavy bombardment wings. However, they retained a standby recconnaissance capability.

Other modifications and changes had been accomplished as operational experience was gained. The most visible of these was the elimination of all defensive armament except the tail guns during the Featherweight III program. The original concept with Featherweight II was to remove most of the crew comfort equipment and other gear deemed nonessential in order to lighten the aircraft. But experience with the gunnery system had shown it to be maintenance intensive, and reliability standards were never met. Reasoning that the greater speed and altitude figures that could be achieved by a lighter aircraft were a better defense than unreliable guns, the decision was made to remove all defensive armament and its associated equipment with the exception of the tail guns. This was known as Featherweight III. The modification was performed on some of the B/RB-36D, E, F, H, and all B-36J aircraft. In fact, the last fourteen B-36Js were originally produced to Featherweight III standards. The program was a success, because no fighter of that era could reach a B-36 with Featherweight III modifications in altitude. If a fighter came close to the altitude of the B-36, the bomber would make a turn, and the fighter would stall out trying to stay with it.

Operationally, the B-36 fleet laid the groundwork for many of the programs that SAC would use for the rest of its career. Overseas deployments and ground alerts were just two activities that would carry into the future of the command. Officially 385 B-36 aircraft were delivered to the Air Force, but that figure does not reflect redesignations. For example, twenty-two B-36A airframes were converted to the RB-36E configuration, and most of the B-36D aircraft started life as B-36Bs.

Although the B-36 was operational on a combat ready status for just over ten years (November 1948 to February 1959) it filled a gap in the defense of this country. For a large part of the 1950s, it was the only method of delivering nuclear weapons to global targets, and as such it constituted the entirety of the deterrent force. So teething problems and near cancellations notwithstanding, when the last B-36J was retired on 12 February, 1959, it could look back on a job well done.

Originally built as a B-36B, this Peacemaker was upgraded to B-36D standards, and with the addition of four jet engines, it exemplifies the final physical form of the design which originated with the "long range bomber program." Subsequent upgrades to the aircraft would involve a number of internal improvements, but only relatively minor external changes would be made. *(USAF)*

AIRCRAFT DESIGN

A B-36A is refuelled at the Convair plant at Fort Worth, Texas. The early propellers with the rounded tips and the lack of defensive armament are evident in this photograph. *(USAF)*

In most respects, the B-36 was fairly conventional and featured a monocoque construction which was standard for the time period in which it was developed. Much attention was given to reducing drag and weight in order to meet range and speed requirements, and this led to some innovative features. The most obvious of these was the pusher engine layout which was the major part of an effort to reduce the frontal area of the twenty-eight cylinder radial engines.

Use of a 3000-PSI hydraulic system resulted in a weight saving as did the use of a 400-cycle, 208-volt, 3-phase electrical system. Flight controls were actuated by servo tabs instead of the hydraulic actuators that would have normally been needed. Integral fuel tanks, using bullet sealing rubber pads mounted on the tanks' exterior, saved even more weight.

Much work was done with new aluminum alloys to reduce weight and retain strength. Particularly notewor-

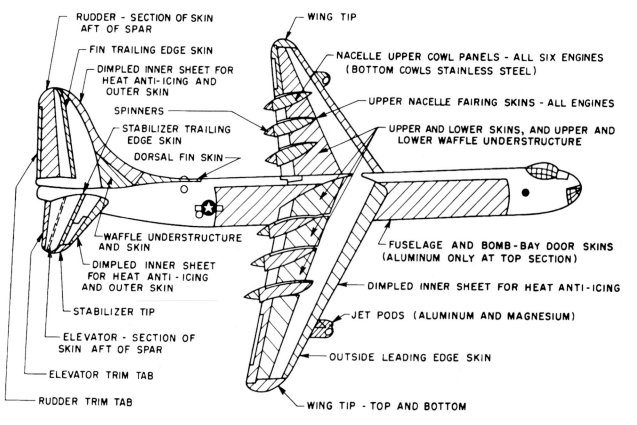

The extensive amount of magnesium used on the B-36 is evident in this drawing. *(USAF)*

FUSELAGE CUTAWAY OF A B-36B SHOWING EQUIPMENT LOCATION

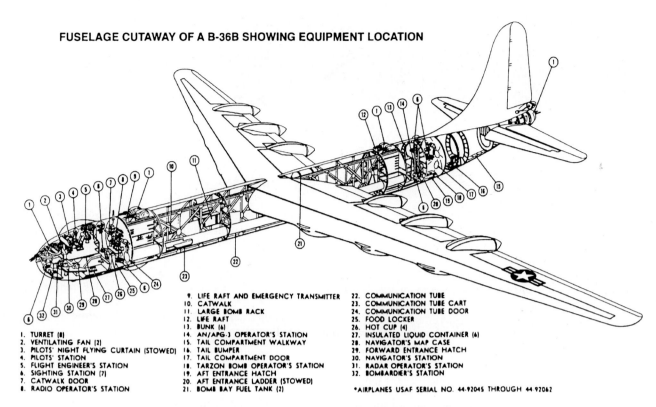

1. TURRET (8)	9. LIFE RAFT AND EMERGENCY TRANSMITTER
2. VENTILATING FAN (2)	10. CATWALK
3. PILOTS' NIGHT FLYING CURTAIN (STOWED)	11. LARGE BOMB RACK
4. PILOTS' STATION	12. LIFE RAFT
5. FLIGHT ENGINEER'S STATION	13. BUNK (6)
6. SIGHTING STATION (7)	14. AN/APG-3 OPERATOR'S STATION
7. CATWALK DOOR	15. TAIL COMPARTMENT WALKWAY
8. RADIO OPERATOR'S STATION	16. TAIL BUMPER
	17. TAIL COMPARTMENT DOOR
	18. TARZON BOMB OPERATOR'S STATION
	19. AFT ENTRANCE HATCH
	20. AFT ENTRANCE LADDER (STOWED)
	21. BOMB BAY FUEL TANK (2)

22. COMMUNICATION TUBE	
23. COMMUNICATION TUBE CART	
24. COMMUNICATION TUBE DOOR	
25. FOOD LOCKER	
26. HOT CUP (4)	
27. INSULATED LIQUID CONTAINER (6)	
28. NAVIGATOR'S MAP CASE	
29. FORWARD ENTRANCE HATCH	
30. NAVIGATOR'S STATION	
31. RADAR OPERATOR'S STATION	
32. BOMBARDIER'S STATION	

*AIRPLANES USAF SERIAL NO. 44-92045 THROUGH 44-92062

ON B-36D AND LATER MODELS THE LIFE RAFTS, TAIL BUMPER AND TARZON BOMB STATION WERE ELIMINATED

thy was the extensive use of magnesium in areas requiring less strength. Much of the external skin of the aircraft was magnesium which saved nearly a ton of weight over using comparable aluminum panels. The shift from the huge single main landing gear wheels to a four-wheel truck saved 2,600 pounds and opened up numerous additional runways to the B-36. Although the retractable gun turrets added weight, the reduction in drag was worth the extra weight of the retraction mechanism.

The propellers, which were nineteen feet in diameter, were automatically synchronized and fully reversible so that they could be used to assist braking during the landing rollout. However, problems were encountered with the pusher design, because the propellers were affected by turbulent airflow over the wing. Further the vibration from the proximity of the props also caused fatigue problems with the flaps.

An interesting method was used to load conventional bombs into the huge bomb bays. Rather than use a lift truck or similar piece of equipment, a series of holes was built into the top of the fuselage over the bomb bays. A C-6 Hoist Unit with an electric winch was placed atop the aircraft. Cables were then let down into the bomb bay through the holes, and the bombs were hoisted into position using the winch. (See page 55.) Bombs weighing in excess of 4,000 pounds were loaded using a hydraulic lift dolly positioned on the ground under the bomb bay.

This drawing shows the location and capacity of the tanks containing consumables. *(USAF)*

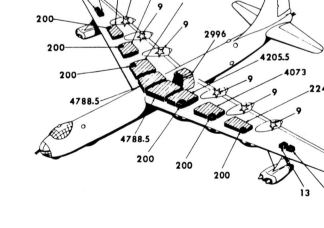

▨ Fuel (Gal)

█ Oil (Gal)

☆ Water Alcohol (Gal)

PRODUCTION VARIANTS

The sixth B-36A shows the lack of defensive armament common to all B-36As. Also note the early football style radio compass loop antenna under the nose. **(General Dynamics)**

B-36A

The twenty-two B-36A aircraft were delivered with Pratt & Whitney R 4360-25 engines, each of which delivered 3,000 horsepower to the 19-foot full-feathering and reversible propellers. The maximum fuel load was 26,745 gallons of avgas, and the bomb bays could accommodate up to 72,000 pounds of munitions. Maximum take-off weight was 310,380 pounds, and this was reached with a 24,121-gallon fuel load and 10,000 pounds of bombs. An aircraft with this load had a tactical range (radius) of 3,880 miles, but with the full load of 72,000 pounds of bombs, the radius was only 2,100 miles. This reduction in radius was due to the fact that the fuel load had to be reduced in order to stay under maximum gross weight. With no bombs aboard and full tanks, the B-36A could fly for 9,136 miles on ferry flights. At a combat weight of 212,800 pounds, the B-36A flew at 345 mph at 31,600 feet, and the service ceiling was 39,100 feet.

The B-36A was equipped with the AN/APQ-23 bombing and navigation radar, sliding bomb bay doors, and no defensive armament. These aircraft equipped the 7th Bomb Group (redesignated 7th Bomb Wing in 1951) at Carswell AFB, Texas, and they were used for testing

This model shows the proposed configuration for the B-36C. The engines were to be the R-4360 equipped with a variable discharge turbine (VDT) supercharger. The engines were still located near the trailing edge of the wing in order to keep drag low, and long shafts were installed to transmit power to the tractor propellers. Problems encountered in trying to mate the VDT supercharger to the engine resulted in the cancellation of the B-36C. **(Jones collection via AAHS)**

and training only. This was because the equipment fit was not completed to full combat production standards.

The first B-36A, 44-92004, made a one-time flight to Wright-Patterson AFB, Ohio, for static testing and was only fitted with minimal equipment. B-36A serial numbers ran from 44-92004 through 44-92025, and they were joined by the sole YB-36A, 42-13571, when the fleet of A models (less 44-92004) were converted to the RB-36E configuration.

B-36B

The basic configuration of the B-36B's airframe was identical to that of the previous B-36A, with the only differences being mostly in equiment fit. The engines were upgraded to the R-4360-41, which was rated at 3,500 horsepower. This increased performance so that speed at combat weight improved to 381 mph, and the service ceiling went up to 42,500 feet.

The AN/APQ-24 bombing and navigational radar was used, and the APG-3 tail gun radar was installed. B-36Bs were fitted with a full compliment of sixteen 20-mm cannons for defense, and the bomb bay doors were made wide enough to accomodate existing nuclear weapons.

A total of two 43,000-pound "Grand Slam" conventional bombs could be carried, and eighteen B-36Bs (44-92045 through 44-92062) were equipped to carry and guide the 13,000-pound VB-13 Tarzon bombs.

A total of seventy-three B-36Bs were built with the serial numbers running from 44-92026 through 44-92098. However, eleven of the aircraft were converted to B/RB-36D standards before they were accepted by the Air Force. This led to confusion, because Convair continued to refer to these as B-36Bs on their records.

B-36C

It was intended that the B-36C would be fitted with R-4360-51 engines with the Variable Displacement Turbine (VDT) supercharger. Although these engines would have been mounted in the same positions as on previous models, they would have been changed to a tractor configuration through the use of long extension shafts. Everything else would have been the same as on the B-36B.

Because of the insurmountable problems that developed when mating the engine with the VDT supercharger, no B-36Cs were ever built.

The final configuration of the B-36 is illustrated by this late production B-36D as it lifts off the runway at Carswell AFB. While there were many equipment changes to come in later variants, the only readily visible one was the deletion of the nose guns during Featherweight III program. **(USAF)**

B-36D

In response to a call for more performance, the B-36D was fitted with four J47-GE-19 turbojet engines which were mounted in pairs outboard of reciprocating engines 1 and 6. The J47 was rated at 5,200 pounds of static thrust, and in combination with the R-4360-41 radials, the performance was increased appreciably. The aircraft was now capable of 406 miles per hour at 32,600 feet, and it had a service ceiling of 43,800 feet. Later, when selected Ds were put through the Featherweight III program, the speed increased to 418 miles per hour.

The maximum weight for take off increased to 357,500 pounds, and the addition of a bomb bay tank increased fuel capacity to 33,000 gallons. Internal equipment included the K-1 bombing system (later upgraded to the K-3), and this combined both visual and radar aiming capability within the same system. A single operator could then handle the radar and bombing work load.

The initial tail radar was the older APG-3, but the later AN/APG-32 system was added during the production run and retrofitted to existing aircraft. However, because the external appearance of both systems was identical, no visual difference could be discerned.

The bomb bay doors were changed from the sliding type (essentially the same as those used on the B-24) to a snap action door actuated by a hydraulic piston that took only two seconds to cycle open or closed. The tail bumper that had equipped the B-36A and B variants was deleted, and the flight control surfaces were changed to

metal instead of the original fabric. This modification was retrofitted to all of the earlier versions as well.

Only twenty-two B-36Ds were built as such from the start. All others were converted from B-36B airframes at Convair's San Diego plant. Original construction B-36Ds were numbered from 49-2647 through 49-2668. A total of thirty-six B-36Ds went through the Featherweight III program. These included 44-92026, 44-92027, 44-92028, 44-92036, 44-92039, 44-92040, 44-92041, 44-92042, 44-92044, 44-92045, 44-92046, 44-92049, 44-92052, 44-92053, 44-92055, 44-92061, 44-92062, 44-92063, 44-92066, 44-92073, 44-92076, 44-92082, 44-92085, 44-92095, 44-92096, 49-2647, 49-2648, 49-2650, 49-2651, 49-2654, 49-2655, 49-2656, 49-2663, 49-2664, 49-2665, and 49-2667.

B-36E

There were no B-36E bombers. The only E models were the RB-36E reconnaissance variant. (See below.)

B-36F

The B-36F was equipped with the R-4360-53 engine which generated 3,800 horsepower, and these, combined with the four J47 jet engines, raised the speed to 417 miles per hour, and the service ceiling to 44,000 feet.

The K-3A bombing system and the AN/APG-32 tail radars were standard, and chaff dispensers were added in

B-36H, 51-5731, has been through the Featherweight III program as indicated by the lack of nose guns.

(Brown via Menard)

the aft fuselage. Later airframes in the B-36F series were equipped with the AN/APG-32A tail radar which used the twin antenna radomes and larger radome fairing.

A total of thirty-four B-36F aircraft were built and assigned serial numbers 49-2669 through 49-2675, 49-2677 through 49-2683, 49-2685, and 50-1064 through 50-1082. The following B-36Fs went through the Featherweight III program: 49-2669, 50-1064, 50-1065, and 50-1081.

B-36G

The B-36G designation was originally given to the swept wing, eight-jet version that was later redesignated the YB-60. It is described and illustrated elsewhere in this book.

B-36H

Equipment fitted in the B-36H was virtually identical to that in the B-36F except for the second flight engineer's station added to the flight deck. Lessons learned from earlier variants contributed greatly to the reliability of operation, and components of the radar system were relocated to the pressurized compartment of the aircraft, thereby facilitating in-flight maintenance.

Performance figures included a top speed of 416 miles per hour and a service ceiling of 44,000 feet. After the Featherweight III modification, these figures rose to 423 miles per hour and 47,000 feet respectively. The twin radomes were still used for the tail radar, but later H models were equipped with the AN/APG-41A radar system. Although this was externally identical to the set it replaced, it was much more capable.

A total of eighty-three B-36H aircraft were built with serial numbers starting at 50-1083 through 50-1097, then 51-5699 through 51-5742. The last batch was assigned numbers 52-1343 to 52-1366. The following aircraft

went through the Featherweight III program: 50-1083, 50-1084, 50-1086, 50-1091, 50-1093, 50-1094, 51-5669 through 51-5704, 51-5708, 51-5711, 51-5713 through 51-5718, 51-5720 through 51-5728, 51-5730 through 51-5742, 52-1343 through 52-1356, and 52-1359 through 52-1366.

B-36J

Externally, the B-36J was identical to the H, but several important changes were made that improved the aircraft's capability. A new fuel tank was added to the wings outboard of the pylons for the jet engines. These tanks held an additional 1,385 gallons each, thus bringing the total fuel capacity to 36,396 gallons of avgas. As a matter of interest, there was no separate fuel system for the jet engines on the B-36 fleet, and the jets burned avgas right along with the reciprocating engines! (Indeed, the author, who flew the B-47, recalls that avgas was one of the emergency fuels listed in the B-47 tech order as acceptable for the J47 engine. However, there was the proviso that the engines may have to be retrimmed to obtain maximum thrust. There was also a concern about lead deposits in the burner cans that would increase the amount of time spent on cleaning them.)

The second modification to the J variant was a stronger landing gear that allowed the maximum weight to increase to 410,000 pounds. The additional weight, with no change in available power, meant that the speed dropped slightly to 411 miles per hour at combat weight.

While the B-36J production run was in progress, the Featherweight III project was implemented to lighten the aircraft, and the last fourteen B-36J airframes were completed to Featherweight III standards as built. All earlier J variants were converted to this configuration as well. The Featherweight III B-36J was capable of 418 miles per hour and had a service ceiling of 43,600 feet. A total of thirty-three B-36Js were built and were assigned tail numbers 52-2210 through 52-2226 and 52-2812 through 52-2827.

B-36J, 52-2827, was the last of the line, being the final B-36 of any type to be built. Here it lifts off the runway at Carswell AFB, Texas to join the inventory. After Air Force acceptance on 10 August, 1954, this aircraft was delivered to the 42nd Bomb Wing at Loring Air Force Base, Maine, on the 14th of August. This aircraft is now undergoing restoration at Fort Worth, and it is one of only four remaining for display. *(General Dynamics)*

MODEL	DESIGN G.W. (LBS)	PRESSURIZED CREW COMPARTMENTS	CREW	ENGINEER'S STATION	RECIP ENGINES	WING FUEL TANKS	GUN TURRETS	BOMB BAYS	BOMBING SYSTEM
B-36D	357,500	2	15	SINGLE	R4360-41	8	8	4	K( ) & UNIVERSAL
B-36D-II	357,500	2	15	SINGLE	R4360-41	8	8	4	K( ) & UNIVERSAL
B-36D-III	357,500	2	13	SINGLE	R4360-41	8	1	4	K( ) & UNIVERSAL
B-36F	357,500	2	15	SINGLE	R4360-53	8	8	4	K( ) & UNIVERSAL
B-36F-II	357,500	2	15	SINGLE	R4360-53	8	8	4	K( ) & UNIVERSAL
B-36F-III	357,500	2	13	SINGLE	R4360-53	8	1	4	K( ) & UNIVERSAL
B-36H	357,500	2	15	DUAL	R4360-53	8	8	4	K( ) & UNIVERSAL
B-36H-II	357,500	2	15	DUAL	R4360-53	8	8	4	K( ) & UNIVERSAL
B-36H-III	357,500	2	13	DUAL	R4360-53	8	1	4	K( ) & UNIVERSAL
B-36J	410,000	2	13	DUAL	R4360-53	10	1	4	K( ) & UNIVERSAL
RB-36D & E	357,500	3	22	SINGLE	R4360-41	8	8	2	CONV. & UNIVERSAL
RB-36D & E-II	357,500	3	22	SINGLE	R4360-41	8	8	3	CONV. & UNIVERSAL
RB-36D & E-III	357,500	3	19	SINGLE	R4360-41	8	1	3	CONV. & UNIVERSAL
RB-36F	357,500	3	22	SINGLE	R4360-53	8	8	2	CONV. & UNIVERSAL
RB-36F-II	357,500	3	22	SINGLE	R4360-53	8	8	3	CONV. & UNIVERSAL
RB-36F-III	357,500	3	19	SINGLE	R4360-53	8	1	3	CONV. & UNIVERSAL
RB-36H	357,500	3	22	DUAL	R4360-53	8	8	2	CONV. & UNIVERSAL
RB-36H-II	357,500	3	22	DUAL	R4360-53	8	8	3	CONV. & UNIVERSAL
RB-36H-III	357,500	3	19	DUAL	R4360-53	8	1	3	CONV. & UNIVERSAL
GRB-36D-III	357,500	3	19	SINGLE	R4360-41	8	1	2	NOT UTILIZED

This table summarizes the main differences between the bomber variants beginning with the B-36D, and all of the reconnaissance versions of the Peacemaker. The Roman numeral II or III indicates the Featherweight program. Featherweight II did not remove the guns, while Featherweight III removed all but the tail turret. *(USAF)*

The early reconnaissance configuration is shown on this RB-36D. Note the three ECM antennas located on bomb bay 4. These would later be moved aft to allow the bomb bay to carry conventional and nuclear weapons. The covers for the camera windows can be seen just aft of the large forward radome and are a lighter color than the surrounding area of the aircraft.
(General Dynamics)

RB-36 Reconnaissance Versions

When SAC expressed a desire for a strategic reconaissance aircraft to augment its bomber fleet, the airframe of the B-36 seemed to offer an answer for that requirement. As a result, after the last B-36B came down the production line, the next aircraft, 44-92088, was built for the RB mission. It was originally completed without the jet pods, but they were added when the B-36Bs were converted to B-36D standards. Reconnaissance variants of the Peacemaker were built in four versions, and these included the RB-36D, E, F, and H which received basically the same improvements as the bomber versions with the corresponding suffixes.

All RB-36s had bomb bay number 1 (about sixteen feet long) converted to a pressurized compartment capable of housing fourteen cameras for photo reconnaissance work. One of these cameras had a 48-inch focal length lens allowing for extremely detailed pictures. The photo technician who operated the cameras also had a small darkroom available, so some film could be developed before the aircraft returned to its base.

Bomb bay number 2 was equipped to carry eighty AN-M46 100-pound photo flash bombs for night photography. They were equipped with a mechanical time delay fuse so the flash would occur at a specific altitude over the target. Bomb bay number 3 was usually reserved for a dropable 3,000-gallon fuel tank.

Bomb bay number 4 held the ferret ECM gear used by the three ECM operators who were located in the aft pressurized compartment. This gear allowed the operators to receive, analyze, and locate radars that "painted" the aircraft as it proceeded along its route. These routes were planned along the periphery (and sometimes over) the country to be investigated, and as the radar network responded to the penetration of local air space, the signals were recorded and the transmitting sites located.

Aircraft performance was a near match for the comparable bomber versions, but averaged slightly better than the bomber early in the mission compared to a fully loaded bomber and slightly less than the bomber near the end of the mission, because there was less expended weight. Although no official performance figures were released, it is safe to say that the ceiling for a Feather-

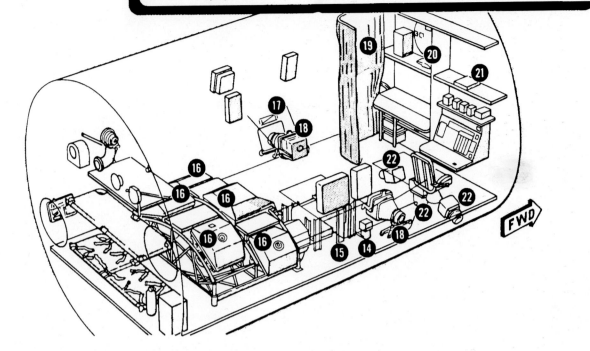

14. Photo Cell Trip Unit	19. Dark Room
15. Vertical Camera Mount	20. Tool Kit
16. Multi Cameras	21. Blowout Safety Strap Stowage
17. Side Oblique Camera Stowage Support	22. Trimetrogon Cameras
18. Side Oblique Camera	

The camera compartment on the RB-36 contained the cameras and positions for the camera operators. Sliding doors covered the camera windows when they were not in use. When the side oblique cameras were in use, a safety harness was worn by the operators in case a window blew out. (USAF)

weight III RB-36F or H was well above 50,000 feet, especially late in the mission when the aircraft was operating at lighter weights. Using endurance power settings, an RB-36 was able to stay aloft for over fifty-one hours as demonstrated during a factory endurance test in 1951.

Midway through the 1950s, SAC shifted the reconnaissance mission to other resources and started to modify the RB-36 fleet to carry conventional and nuclear bombs. To this end, the RB-36 airframes were modified to retain the camera compartment, but bomb bays 2, 3, and 4 were made identical to those of the bomber versions. This was accomplished by moving the ferret ECM gear to the aft fuselage and installing racks capable of carrying the larger bombs. By October 1955, all of the strategic reconnaissance wings had been redesignated strategic bombardment wings, and they retained only a latent reconnaissance capability.

Of the RB-36Ds, seventeen were built from the start as such, and they were assigned serial numbers 49-2686 through 49-2702. Additionally, seven B-36B airframes were converted to the RB-36D configuration. The following RB-36Ds went through the Featherweight III modification: 44-92089, 44-92090, 44-92092, 44-92094, 49-2687, 49-2692, 49-2694, 49-2695, 49-2696, 49-2701, and 49-2702. In addition, the following ten RB-36Ds were equipped to carry the RF-84K and were redesignated GRB-36D: 44-92090, 44-92092, 44-92094, 49-2687, 49-2692, 49-2694, 49-2695, 49-2696, 49-2701, and 49-2702.

All of the twenty-two RB-36Es were converted from the sole YB-36 (42-13571) and twenty-one B-36As. The following RB-36Es went through the Featherweight III program: 42-13571 (YB-36), 44-92006, 44-92007, 44-92009, 44-92011, and 44-92012.

There were twenty-four RB-36Fs built, and all were produced as such from the start. These aircraft received serial numbers 49-2703 through 49-2721 and 50-1098 through 50-1102. Of these, only 50-1101 received Featherweight III modifications.

This RB-36E is shown with the Circle X tail markings of the 5th Strategic Reconnaissance Wing at Travis AFB, California. The X identifies the 5th SRW, while the circle was used by the 15th Air Force. These markings are provided to modelers in the latest release of the Monogram 1/72nd scale kit. (U. S. Air Force Museum)

One of ten RB-36Ds converted to the production GRB configuration, this aircraft shows the rendezvous antenna on the top of the fuselage. Note how the ECM antennas have been moved aft of their original position on bomb bay 4, and they are now just below the national insignia on the lower aft fuselage. This change was directed by T. O. 1B-36(R)-216 when SAC decided to give the RB-36s a primary bombing mission. (General Dynamics)

The most numerous reconnaissance variant of the Peacemaker was the RB-36H of which seventy-three were produced. They received serial numbers 50-1103 through 50-1110, 51-5743 through 51-5756, and 52-1367 through 52-1392. Of these, the following RB-36Hs went through the Featherweight III program: 50-1103 through 50-1110, 51-5743 through 51-5748, 51-13723, 51-13734, 51-13735, 51-13738, 51-13739, 52-1386, 52-1387, and 52-1389.

This brand new RB-36H, 52-1384, still has the factory sequence number, 333, on the nose. These sequence numbers were an easy way of identifying aircraft on the assembly line, and they started with the prototype. Therefore, this is the 333rd B-36 to roll out of the Fort Worth factory. (General Dynamics)

DESIGN DERIVATIVES

Although not a bomber, the XC-99 retained the wings and tail surfaces of the B-36. As originally tested, the aircraft was fitted with the large single-wheel main landing gear.
(USAF)

Later, the XC-99 (redesignated C-99) received the four-wheel trucks for the main gear like the B-36 and RB-36 aircraft. Also note the radome that was added to the nose of the aircraft.
(Steeneck via AAHS)

Two B-36 derivatives also became flying prototypes and deserve mention here. Convair completed one XC-99 transport version and delivered it to the Air Force for testing in 1949. The XC-99 used the B-36's engines, wing, and landing gear, and this was mated to a huge double-decked fuselage that could be used to carry up to 100,000 pounds of cargo. The aircraft was used extensively on cargo runs during the Korean War, but even though the cost per ton-mile was lower than other cargo aircraft of that time, the XC-99 proved to be impractical. No single depot could ship enough at one time to fill the load, so this necessitated several short hops to fully load the aircraft. By 1957, the useful airframe life was ex-pended, and the aircraft was retired at Kelly AFB, Texas.

The second derivative came about to address the B-36's lack of speed. Convair proposed sweeping the wings and re-equipping the aircraft with jet engines. Originally this was to have been the B-36G, but due to the major changes, it was redesignated the YB-60 by the Air Force. Two examples were ordered, and testing started in 1952. However, the first YB-60, 49-2676, was found to be inferior to the B-52 in speed, handling, and other characteristics, so the second prototype was never completed. Both airframes were scrapped shortly after formal delivery to the Air Force in 1954.

The B-36G was redesignated the YB-60, however it did not compare well to its competition, the B-52. This resulted in the cancellation of the project.
(General Dynamics)

FIGHTER CONVEYOR PROGRAM

FICON testing was conducted with RB-36F, 49-2707, and a modified F-84F. The bomb bay doors were removed, and this meant that all flights had to be made with the upper aft turret doors open. Otherwise, the air coming up through the bomb bays would enter the aft turret and blow the doors off. Production FICON GRB-36 aircraft were all D models, and they had fairing doors to close the bomb bay completely.
(Williams via AAHS)

One interesting and highly visibile modification associated with the B-36 was the FICON (fighter conveyor) program. This was based on the theory that a large long range aircraft could carry a smaller aircraft with it for self protection or increased reconnaissance capability. After extensive flight testing in 1952 and 1953, a contract was let to modify ten RB-36D airframes so that they could mate in flight with specially equipped RF-84K photo reconnaissance fighters. These aircraft were delivered to SAC in 1955, and they went through a workup to combat ready status during 1956. The project was short lived and was disbanded by mid-1957.

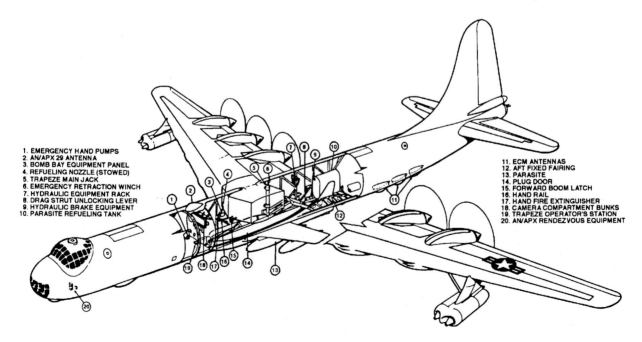

1. EMERGENCY HAND PUMPS
2. AN/APX 29 ANTENNA
3. BOMB BAY EQUIPMENT PANEL
4. REFUELING NOZZLE (STOWED)
5. TRAPEZE MAIN JACK
6. EMERGENCY RETRACTION WINCH
7. HYDRAULIC EQUIPMENT RACK
8. DRAG STRUT UNLOCKING LEVER
9. HYDRAULIC BRAKE EQUIPMENT
10. PARASITE REFUELING TANK

11. ECM ANTENNAS
12. AFT FIXED FAIRING
13. PARASITE
14. PLUG DOOR
15. FORWARD BOOM LATCH
16. HAND RAIL
17. HAND FIRE EXTINGUISHER
18. CAMERA COMPARTMENT BUNKS
19. TRAPEZE OPERATOR'S STATION
20. AN/APX RENDEZVOUS EQUIPMENT

This drawing shows how the RB-36D was modified to carry the RF-84K. With the RF-84K retracted, the bomb bay was sealed off by fairing doors and the vertical tail of the fighter came up through a slot in the concave fixed fairing.
(USAF)

This GRB-36D, 44-29090, began life as a B-36B, then it was converted to an RB-36D and finally to GRB status. Just visible in this underside view is the concave area with the slot for the vertical tail of the RF-84K. Note that for some reason the forward ECM radome has been removed.
(Bishop)

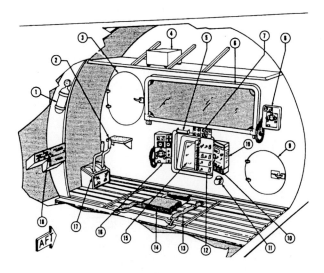

1. PORTABLE OXYGEN BOTTLE	8. OXYGEN AND INTER-PHONE PANEL	14. SEAT
2. STEP	9. COMMUNICATION TUBE DOOR	15. WINDOW
3. BOMB BAY ENTRANCE	10. AUXILIARY CONTROL PANEL	16. INSTRUMENT PANEL
4. AN/APX-29 RECEIVER-TRANSMITTER	11. PRESSURE DUMP VALVE	17. TRAPEZE EMERGENCY HYDRAULIC CONTROLS
5. HAND GRIP	12. MAIN CONTROL PANEL	18. PROTECTIVE EQUIPMENT STOWAGE BIN
6. BUNKS	13. SAFETY HARNESS	19. INSTRUCTION PLACARD
7. LIGHTING CONTROL PANEL		

On the RB-36D aircraft modified for the FICON program, a sighting window and trapeze controls were added to the rear bulkhead of the camera compartment.   *(USAF)*

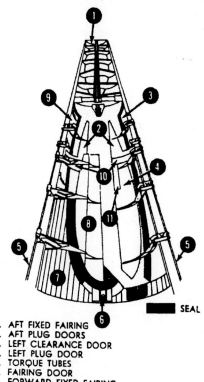

1. AFT FIXED FAIRING
2. AFT PLUG DOORS
3. LEFT CLEARANCE DOOR
4. LEFT PLUG DOOR
5. TORQUE TUBES
6. FAIRING DOOR
7. FORWARD FIXED FAIRING
8. CATWALK PLUG DOOR
9. RIGHT CLEARANCE DOOR
10. YOKE PLUG DOOR
11. POSITIONING JACK PLUG DOOR

■ SEAL

The partially open fairing doors that closed the bomb bay when the RF-84K was not being carried are illustrated in this drawing. The seals were made of flexible rubber in order to fit snugly against the fighter.   *(USAF)*

PROJECT TOM-TOM

The Tom-Tom testing was conducted on the same RB-36F used for FICON testing. The bomb bay doors are still removed, and the radome for the AN/APX-29 rendezvous equipment is still mounted on top of the fuselage. Note the open aft turret.
(General Dynamics)

Similar to the FICON program was Project Tom-Tom. The concept was to develop another method of carrying a fighter aircraft instead of using the bomb bays. This would save the space in the bays for weapons, thus allowing the carrying aircraft to perform its mission as a bomber as well as transporting the fighter. Under Project Tom-Tom, the feasibility of attaching fighters to the wing tips was investigated. An RF-84F was used as the fighter, and a special fitting was installed on the wing tips of both the RF-84F and the RB-36F test aircraft. This would permit the RB-36F to tow the RF-84F for the greater part of the mission. Testing in late 1952 and early 1953 revealed great difficulty, and wing tip vortices affected the stability of the fighter. After one test hop where damage was sustained by both aircraft, the project was terminated.

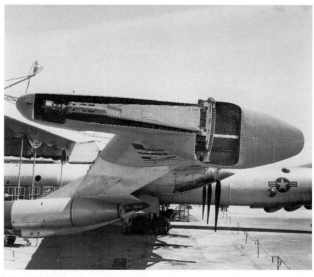

At left is the claw-like hook-up device mounted to the wing of the RF-84 and at right is the attachment rig on the wing tip of the RB-36.
(Both General Dynamics)

Joining the two aircraft on the ground required the use of some scaffolding which mounted a crane. This tedious work is being performed in the photograph above. Below is a close-up of technicians checking the hook-up device. Note the camera on the fighter's wing tip that would record the join-up procedure in flight. (Both General Dynamics)

TEST PROGRAMS

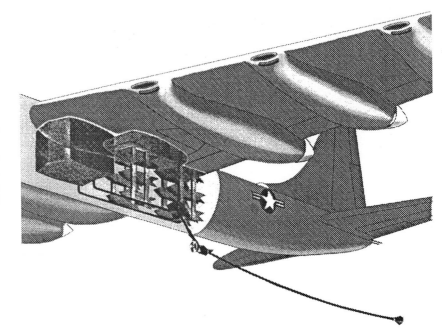

This drawing shows the concept involved in the B-36 tanker attachment. It was a bolt-in retractable reel containing a hose, generator, and basket. The changeover could be completed in twelve hours. *(USAF)*

B-36 Tanker Program

The B-36 was used in a number of interesting test programs, one of which came about in 1952 when the Air Force asked Convair to equip a test aircraft with a probe and drogue refueling system to investigate the feasibility of using the B-36 as a tanker. A removable system was developed that allowed conversion from a bomber to a tanker in twelve hours, and testing in 1952 and 1953 demonstrated that the system did work. However, problems with the slow speed of the B-36, combined with its heavy commitment in the bomber role, precluded further development in this area.

In-flight Nuclear Reactor

One of the most notable test programs in which the B-36 was used was the flight testing of a nuclear reactor. To investigate the possibilities of powering an aircraft with atomic power, a single B-36H, 51-5712, was extensively modified to accept a small reactor in the aft fuselage. Heavy shielding for the crew necessitated the complete redesign of the forward crew compartment, and this changed the look of the airplane considerably. Although the reactor was not used to power the aircraft in any way, much data on the effects of radiation on the airframe and other components was gathered during the forty-seven test flights made by the NB-36H.

One of the more unusual test aircraft to use the B-36 airframe was the NB-36. It was originally B-36H, 51-5712, but it was modified considerably to carry a small nuclear reactor. In order to provide adequate shielding for the crew, the cockpit and nose section had to be completely redesigned. Another photograph of this aircraft appears on page 33 in the color section of this book.
(General Dynamics)

The modified bomb bay doors used to mount the GAM-63 Rascal missile can be seen here. The missile was carried semi-recessed in the aft bay for aerodynamic and drag tests. These were conducted on B-36H, 51-5710, during the summer of 1953.
(General Dynamics)

Missile Carrier Tests

In 1952, a bid was made to make the B-36 a missile carrier. The proposal was to modify some aircraft so that they would be capable of carrying and launching the GAM-63 Rascal missile, but the decision to use the B-47 as the carrier aircraft ended the B-36's involvement. Problems with the missile later caused the cancellation of the entire GAM-63 project in 1958.

Engine Pod Program

In an effort to increase deployablity of the aircraft, large engine pods were developed that could be used to transport fully assembled R-4360 radial engines to deployment bases. Two aerodynamically shaped pods were connected by a cross piece that could be attached to a support in the aircraft's bomb bay. The concept of the program was to allow B-36s to carry spare engines with them during a deployment without having to use additional transport aircraft for them.

These large pods were developed to carry built-up R-4360 engines to deployment bases. They were attached into the forward bomb bay, and they held two engines each. This photograph also provides a good look at the nose glazing and the forward gun turret.
(General Dynamics)

EXTERNAL FINISH & MARKINGS

This B-36B has the red Arctic markings on the outer wing panels and the tail section. Note the tail bumper under the aft fuselage and how the nose of the aircraft is supported on a stand in order to keep the 47-foot high vertical tail from hitting the overhead girders and lights. A sideways cant was also needed to allow the 230-foot wings to clear the 200-foot wide hangar doors. *(USAF)*

The XB-36 and the subsequent B-36A aircraft were left in natural metal, thus revealing the two types of aluminum and the magnesium used for the skin. National insignias were located on the aft fuselage and the top left and bottom right wing surfaces. Large buzz numbers (**BM** plus the last three digits of the tail number) were located on the fuselage sides between the cockpit and wing. For a time the buzz number was also carried under the left outer wing.

Soon after being delivered to the 7th Bomb Group at Carswell Air Force Base, the aircraft were marked with a large triangle on the fin and rudder to designate the unit. The 8th Air Force insignia also made an appearance on the forward sides of the fin.

Geometric tail markings are exemplified by the Triangle S markings on this RB-36H at Ellsworth AFB, South Dakota. The triangle indicates the 8th Air Force, and the S designates the 28th Strategic Reconnaissance Wing. *(USAF)*

The Triangle U tail markings on this B-36H indentify it as belonging to the 11th bomb wing. Also note the squadron colors on the nose gear doors and the jet intakes. The squadron insignia is on the right side of the nose, and the wing insignia would have been on the left side. *(General Dynamics)*

As the B-36B variants were delivered, red Arctic markings started to appear, first as a test, then fleet wide on new aircraft as they were delivered. The red covered the vertical tail, both the upper and lower surfaces of the horizontal tails, and the top and bottom of the wings outboard of engines 1 and 6. Along with the red paint, the **USAF** markings for the bottom left and upper right wings appeared. As with any military paint scheme, there were many exceptions, but these were the general rule.

When the red markings were added, the buzz numbers started to disappear, and they were replaced with **UNITED STATES AIR FORCE** in nine-inch letters on the forward fuselage sides. Then the buzz numbers reappeared on the fuselage sides without the **BM** prefix. Finally, the red markings disappeared, and the triangle reappeared on the tail with a **J** or **U** in the center denoting the 7th or 11th Bomb Wings respectively. The use of large geometric symbols to designate the unit and numbered air force

continued into 1952 with the following symbol/wing assignments:

Carswell AFB	7th BW	Triangle J
	11th BW	Triangle U
Walker AFB	6th BW	Triangle R
Ellsworth AFB	28th BW	Triangle S
Travis AFB	5th SRW	Circle X
Fairchild AFB	92nd BW	Circle W
	99th SRW	Circle I
Ramey AFB	72nd SRW	Square F

The 95th Bomb Wing at Biggs AFB, Texas, and the 42nd Bomb Wing at Loring AFB, Maine, were activated in November 1952 and February 1953 respectively. However, these units were not assigned geometric codes as they were already being phased out by then.

This drawing shows the areas on the top of the aircraft that were painted with anti-skid paint. This gave a slightly roughened texture to the surface. *(USAF)*

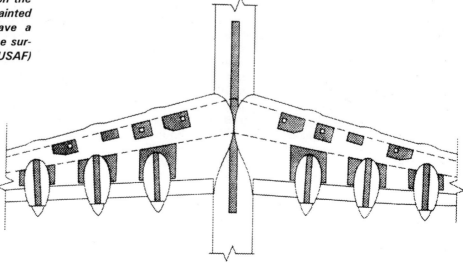

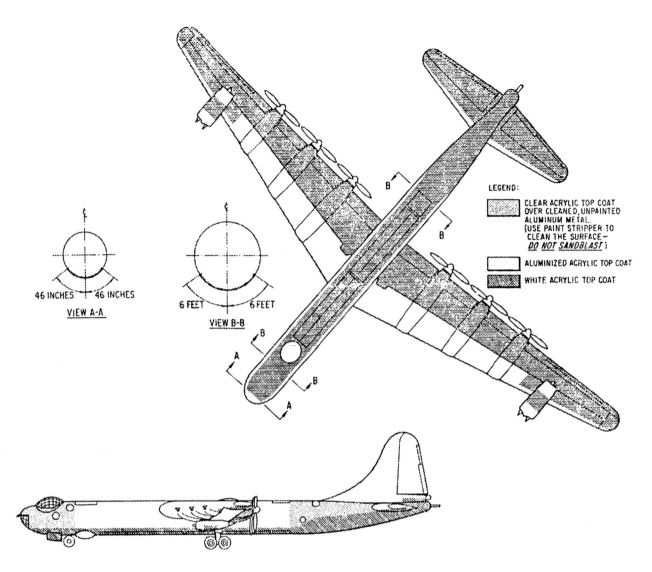

LEGEND:

CLEAR ACRYLIC TOP COAT OVER CLEANED, UNPAINTED ALUMINUM METAL. (USE PAINT STRIPPER TO CLEAN THE SURFACE — *DO NOT SANDBLAST*)

ALUMINIZED ACRYLIC TOP COAT

WHITE ACRYLIC TOP COAT

46 INCHES — 46 INCHES

VIEW A-A

6 FEET — 6 FEET

VIEW B-B

The areas to be covered by white anti-thermal paint and the two types of protective acrylic paint are indicated in this drawing. Note that the major part of the fuselage and the tops of the wings and stabilizers were covered by the aluminized paint. **(USAF)**

At this time, most aircraft were assigned to a specific squadron for maintenance, and the squadron color was often painted on the fin tip and nose gear doors. As the B-36D and later models spread through the fleet, the use of a small **UNITED STATES AIR FORCE** and the last three digits of the serial number on the fuselage side became standard. Additionally, a plain vertical tail with the numbered air force insignia on it was used. The use of squadron colors also continued, with some units painting them on the front of the jet pods with contrasting stripes.

The last significant change in markings occurred during the 1955-56 time frame. The **UNITED STATES AIR FORCE**, which had been painted in small lettering on the side of the fuselage, was replaced with **U. S. AIR FORCE** in 36-inch high letters. The bottom of the aircraft was painted in anti-thermal white to protect the skin from the flash effects of thermonuclear weapons.

Along with the white paint, a protective acrylic paint was applied to the rest of the aircraft to inhibit corrosion. Generally, the paint on the pressurized areas was clear, but that over most of the fuselage and wings was an aluminized paint that covered and obscured the original metal skin. On the painted aircraft, the **USAF** marking on the lower surface of the left wing was deleted. Some units continued to paint their squadron colors on the fin and/or jet pods, but with the arrival of consolodated maintenance, these slowly disappeared.

Individual unit insignias on the nose of the aircraft went through several phases starting with the wing insignia on the left side, and it was sometimes repeated on the right side. Some units had the wing insignia on the left and the squadron insignia on the right, but this was not practiced throughout the fleet. In the early 1950s, it was possible to see aircraft with no insignia at all on the nose. In 1954, the nose insignia became standardized with SAC's "star spangled band" appearing under the SAC crest on the left side of the nose. In most cases, just the band on was on the right side. In other instances, the wing insignia was used on the right band. With the exception of some specialized aircraft, these were the markings that the B-36 fleet carried to the disposal facility at Davis Monthan AFB.

COLOR GALLERY

With a few exceptions, such as the aircraft illustrated on the front cover of this book, B-36 aircraft were not very colorful, nor did they carry elaborate markings. Another exception was the NB-36 which had red, white, and blue trim. It also carried the yellow and red radiation warning symbol on both sides of its vertical tail. *(General Dynamics)*

A B-36B with red Arctic markings takes off from Carswell AFB, Texas. The yellow squadron color is painted on the nose gear doors. This particular aircraft carries the small UNITED STATES AIR FORCE on its forward fuselage sides. *(USAF)*

This B-36B was assigned to the 7th Bomb Group at Carswell AFB during July 1949. It also has the red Arctic markings, and the unit insignia is painted on the nose. Also note the buzz number on the fuselage side. *(USAF via Menard)*

This B-36B from the 7th Bomb Wing sports a triangle on the tail but no letter. The red trim on the fin and nose gear doors indicates squadron assignment. Note that the sliding bomb bay doors partially obscure the buzz numbers when open. (Menard)

This B-36H was assigned to the 11th Bomb Wing as indicated by the geometric Triangle U markings on its tail. The Eighth Air Force insignia is also on the tail, and the unit crest is on the nose. Although there is no squadron color present on the nose gear doors, the jet cowlings have rather elaborate markings. Note also that the last four digits of the serial number are painted on the fuselage sides under the small UNITED STATES AIR FORCE. These markings replaced the previous buzz numbers. (Applegate via Mesko)

These two photographs of a B-36D assigned to the 42nd Bomb Wing show the yellow squadron color painted on the nose gear doors, on the vertical tail in the form of a band, on the jet pod cowlings, and even on the prop spinners. U. S. AIR FORCE is painted on the forward fuselage sides in large letters, and SAC's star spangled band is on the nose. The SAC insignia is on the left side, and the unit crest is on the right. These markings indicate that the photographs were taken between 1954 and 1956, after the geometric and letter symbols had disappeared, but before the addition of anti-thermal white paint on the undersides of the aircraft. (Both Menard)

This Featherweight III B-36J has the jet cowlings in red and the standard anti-thermal white paint on its undersides. The fin cap appears to be black. Note the faired over gun turret and the plate replacing the bomb aimer's window. These were both features on aircraft that had gone through the Featherweight III program. (Nelson via Menard)

B-36J COCKPIT DETAILS & COLORS

Above is the pilot's position in a B-36J. Only flight instruments and the gages for the four jet engines are on the panel. Below is the co-pilot's station which is even less cluttered than the pilot's.

This is the overhead console above the pilot's and co-pilot's seats.

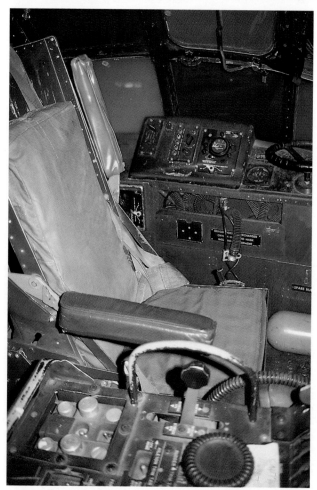

The pilot's seat with its olive drab cushions and the surrounding panels illustrate the normal wear and tear of operations.

This is the co-pilot's seat and the panels which surround it. The center console held the auto pilot controls, trim controls, and electrical switches.

The busiest panel was the flight engineer's panel. In the B-36H and J, there were two engineers. This is the left side of the panel.

The center section of the flight engineer's panel is shown here.

This is the right side of the panel manned by the two flight engineers.

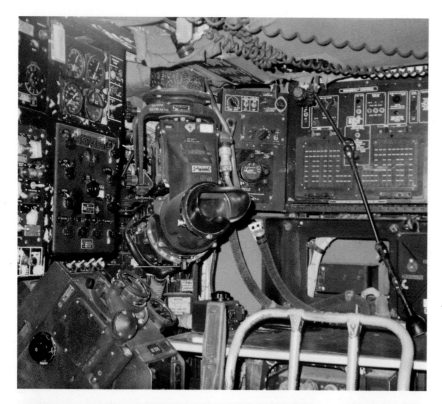

The position occupied by the radar navigator on a B-36J is shown in this view.   (Kinzey)

The navigator's position is located along the left side of the lower forward compartment.

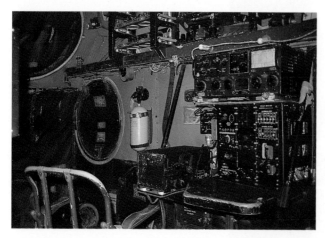

The radio operator's position was located to the rear of and below the flight deck. In addition to nor-mal radio operator duties, the defensive ECM equipment was also the responsibility of this crew position.

This is the radar scope and controls for the AN/APG-41 tail radar. This equipment was located at the right rear of the aft compartment facing outboard.

RB-36 INTERIOR DETAILS & COLORS

Very few photographs have ever been published that show personnel manning their positions in an RB-36 during the time the aircraft was in service. The photographs on this page and the next are very rare color photographs taken in an RB-36 of the 5th Strategic Reconnaissance Wing based at Travis Air Force Base, California. This unit was part of the Fifteenth Air Force. In this view, 1LT Donald Chapman (left) and 2LT Guy Smith man the flight engineer's panel. (USAF)

In the lower nose compartment are four crewmen. The nose glazing of the aircraft can be seen in the background to the left. 1LT James Shively, seated in the left foreground, is the navigator. The photo navigator, Captain William Merrill, is above him and to the left. A1C Albert Brown is the nose gunner and weather observer, and to the right is Captain Franklin O'Donald, the radar observer. (USAF)

This is part of the photo compartment where the cameras are controlled. At the control panel is A1C Carl Haley, one of the camera operators assigned to the RB-36.   *(USAF)*

SSG John McCarl sits in the radio operator's position on the RB-36. Note the sighting blister in the upper right corner of the photograph.   *(USAF)*

In the rear pressurized compartment or "rear office" of the RB-36 are two electronic warfare officers. Captain Harold Weiner is on the left and Captain William Dempsey is on the right. In the background is the rear gunner, SSG Albert Whipple.   *(USAF)*

DIMENSIONS

MEASUREMENT	ACTUAL	1/144TH SCALE	1/72ND SCALE	1/48th SCALE
Wingspan	230'	19.1"	38.3"	57.5"
Length (Overall, including guns)	167' 1"	13.9"	27.8"	41.7"
Height	46' 10"	3.9"	7.8"	11.7"

The following drawings show 5 views of an early B-36F with the AN/APG-32 tail radar. Additional side views of an RB-36F prior to T.O. 1B-36(R)-216 are furnished. The drawings are done in 1/288 scale. Drawings in 1/144 and 1/72 may be obtained by enlarging 200% and 400% respectively.

DETAIL & SCALE FIVE-VIEW SCALE DRAWINGS

Detail & Scale Copyright Drawing by Wayne Wachsmuth

B-36F FRONT VIEW

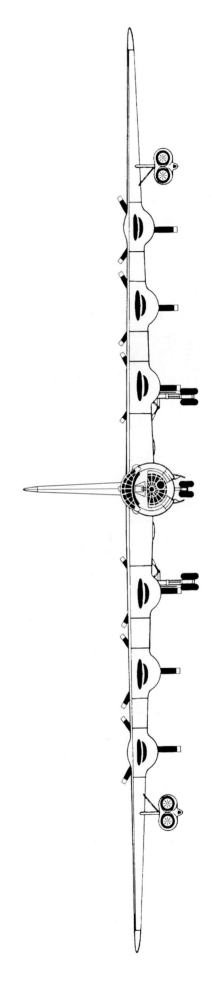

B-36F TOP VIEW

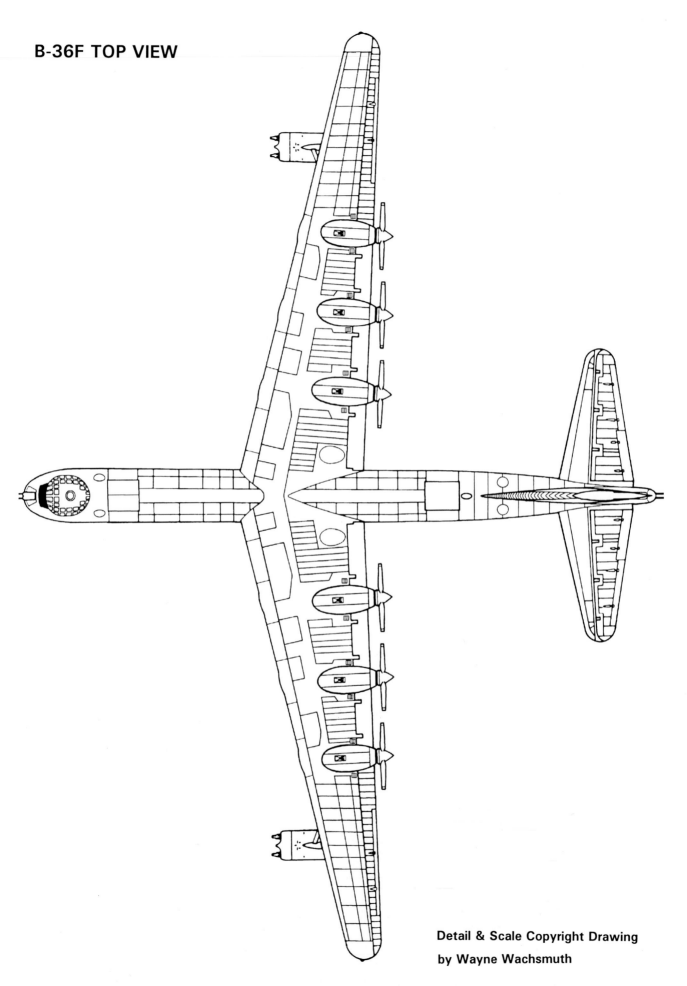

Detail & Scale Copyright Drawing
by Wayne Wachsmuth

B-36F BOTTOM VIEW

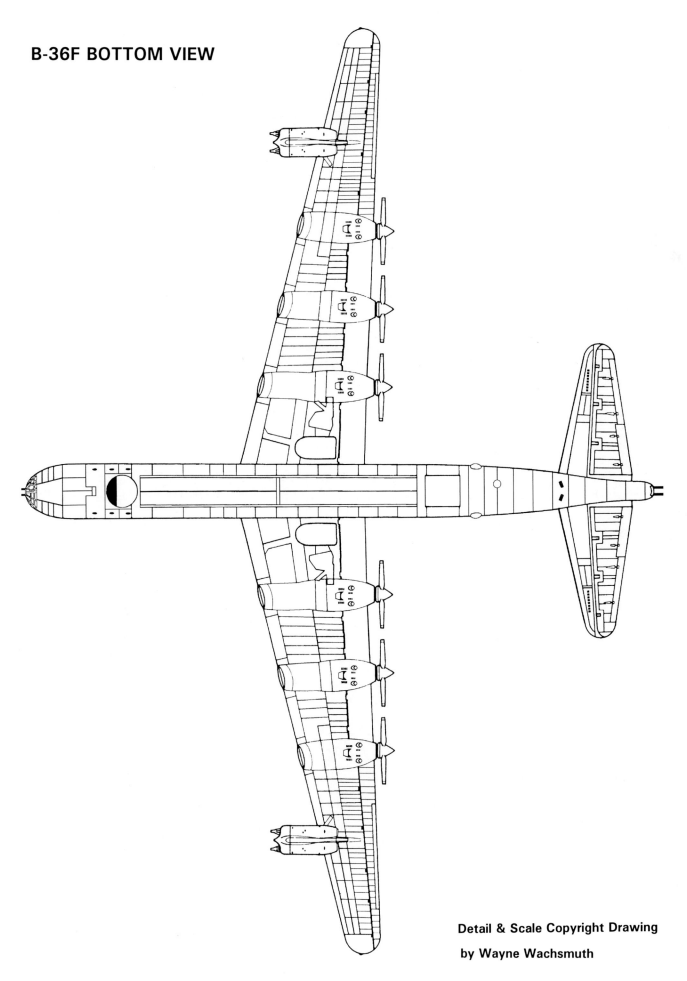

Detail & Scale Copyright Drawing

by Wayne Wachsmuth

43

B-36F RIGHT SIDE VIEW

B-36F LEFT SIDE VIEW

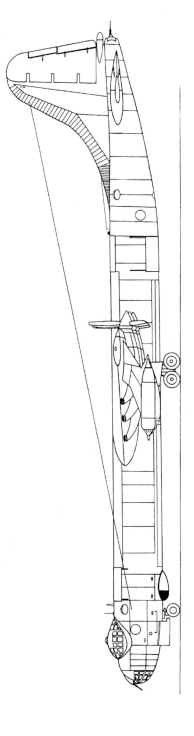

THE TWO DRAWINGS ON THIS PAGE ILLUSTRATE THE RB-36F PRIOR TO THE CHANGE
DIRECTED BY T.O. 1B-36(R)-216.

RB-36F RIGHT SIDE VIEW

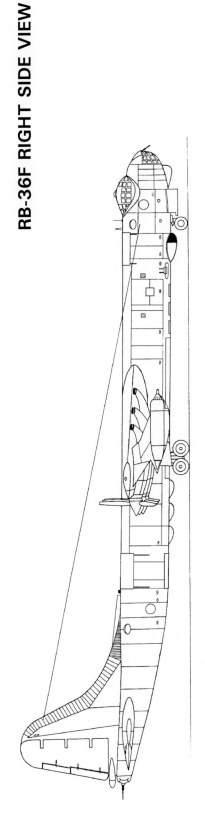

RB-36F LEFT SIDE VIEW

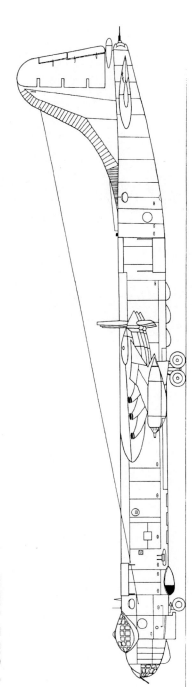

Detail & Scale Copyright Drawing by Wayne Wachsmuth

PEACEMAKER DETAILS

LANDING GEAR DETAILS

NOSE LANDING GEAR DETAILS

The nose gear is mounted on a conventional strut with the steering unit located just above the oleo. *(Kinzey)*

The aft end of the nose wheel well is shown here, The strut and attached hydraulic lines are visible. *(Kinzey)*

This close-up of the nose wheel shows the spoke pattern to good effect. *(K. Wachsmuth)*

The entrance hatch, boarding ladder, the door pickup arm, and the door closing linkage are all visible in this photograph of the forward end of the nose wheel well.

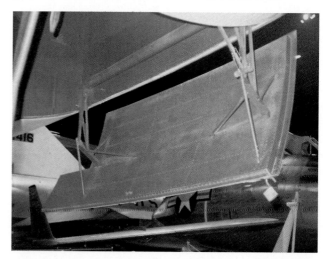

This is the interior of the left nose gear door and its bracing. The right door is similar except that the segment which extends aft is smaller. *(Kinzey)*

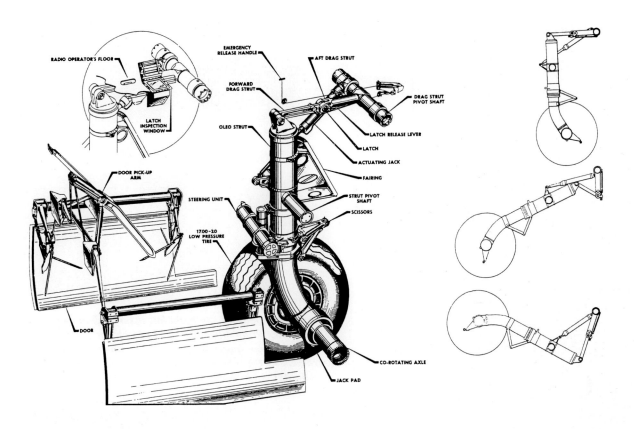

This drawing shows the nose gear components and their relationship.

(USAF via Cripliver)

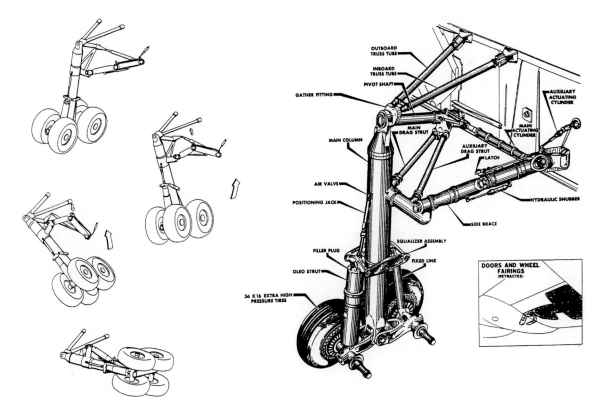

The components and the method of attachment of the production main landing gear are illustrated in this drawing.

(USAF via Cripliver)

MAIN LANDING GEAR DETAILS

This is the interior of the outer left main landing gear well. The various struts and tubes that attach the main gear to the main wing spar are visible. The small door hanging vertically in the photo would normally swing farther aft and lie flat against the lower wing surface.

The four-wheel main gear employed two hinged axle beams that transmitted up and down motion through a fixed link and oleo strut to the equalizer assembly on the main strut. In this photograph, the oleo is protected by a canvas cover. Note the early wheel design used on the B-36A and B aircraft and also on the B-36D and RB-36E variants which were converted from these earlier versions.
(USAF)

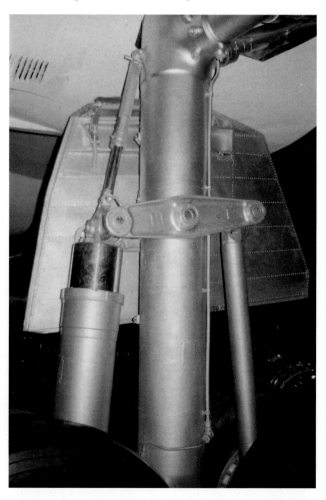

The later design for the main wheel can be seen here. This type was also used on B-36D aircraft beginning with 49-2647.

A close-up of the main strut shows the oleo and the positioning jack just above it. Details of the equalizer assembly and fixed link can be seen along with the tubing runs for the brakes.

EXPERIMENTAL LANDING GEAR DETAILS

Left: The huge size of the original main landing gear is evident in this photograph. The footprint weight was so great that only three bases in the United States had runways capable of handling it. **(USAF Museum)**

Above: A tracked gear was attempted to lower the footprint weight, but complexity, weight, and a twenty-percent penalty in takeoff distance made it impracticable. This is the nose gear as viewed from the left side. Note the complexity of the system, although the nose gear did not even have brakes. **(General Dynamics)**

Below: Each of the main gear had a dual track system. Note the brakes at the forward end of the gear. **(USAF)**

The Pratt & Whitney R-4360 engine was massive in design and had multiple rows of cylinders that were arranged diagonally. *(USAF Museum)*

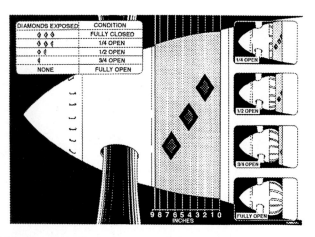

This drawing illustrates the design of the air plug. Its function was to control the flow of cooling air through the nacelle. The diamonds were red with a black outline, and they provided references for the scanners who informed the flight deck as to the amount of the opening for each plug. *(USAF)*

Ease of access was not a strong point when working on the engines. This view also shows the exhaust slots around the prop spinners for the anti-icing air. *(USAF)*

The numbers on the flap segments and engine nacelles are visible here. These were used to aid the scanners in the lower aft turret blisters. The air plugs used to control air flow through each nacelle are also visible with the plug on number 5 extended two diamonds or six inches. *(USAF)*

The later maintenance practice was to build up the engine into a "power egg" that could be changed rapidly.
(USAFHRC)

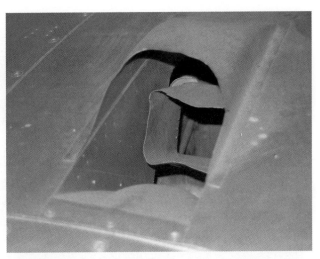

On top of each engine nacelle was a rearward facing outlet for the anti-icing air dump valve.

The intercooler shutters were located at the sides of each engine nacelle on top of the wings. They were flush with the wing surface when they were closed.

At the tip of each propeller blade was the exhaust outlet for the prop anti-icing air. This was present on both the early propellers with the rounded tips and the later props with the square tips as shown here.

The oil cooler door and cooling louvers on the bottom of the engine nacelle can be seen here.   (USAF Museum)

JET ENGINES

Above: The front of the jet engine pod can be seen here with the intake shutters in the closed position. Note the taxi light mounted into the bottom of the pod. *(Menard)*

Left: This General Electric J47 has the accessory section removed and is mounted on a shop stand for maintenance. *(USAF Museum)*

Moveable tabs were mounted on the tail pipe of each jet engine. These were used to trim the operating temperature of the J47.

BOMB BAYS

A large hydraulic lift bearing a 43,000-pound bomb is placed under the forward bay of a B-36A for test loading. The lift is partly raised into the bay. Note the configuration of the sliding bomb bay doors.   (USAF Museum)

The snap action doors on the B-36D and later models took only two seconds to open or close.

In the lower half of the turret compartment there is a walkway which spans the radome and provides a mount for the antenna.

These door actuators are at the forward end of bomb bay 1. The lower part of the forward turret compartment can be seen in the background.

The communication tunnel along the left side of the bomb bays had windows in it at intervals to permit scanning for hung munitions.   (Kinzey)

The divider between the forward and aft bays contains door actuators, hydraulic reservoirs, and accumulators.

The bomb bay divider also held the single point refueling receptacle and the lower white navigation light. This photograph was taken from the left side of the aircraft.

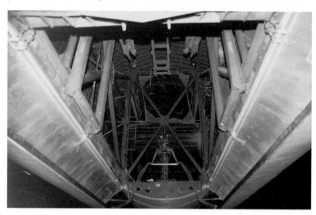

This photograph of the aft end of bomb bay 4 shows the rear actuators and the aft turret compartment. When the bomb bay doors were opened, the increased air pressure would blow the aft turret doors off unless they were also opened simultaneously.

Mounted in the forward and aft bays was a universal bomb rack capable of holding large munitions. Both conventional or nuclear/thermonuclear weapons could be carried on this rack.

The bomb racks for conventional munitions were attached to ladder-like fittings at the sides of the bays.   (Kinzey)

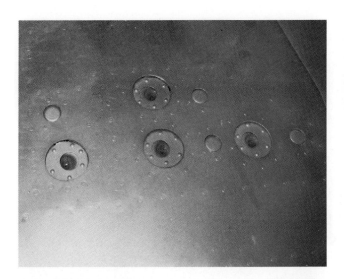
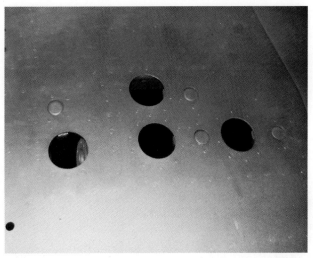

On top of the fuselage above the bomb bays was a series of holes through which cables could be lowered. The cables could then be used with a winch to hoist conventional bombs into position. The holes were about three inches in diameter and were fitted with small round doors to close the hole when not in use. Each door had a depression in the center that served as a finger hold to close it. A release button was located near each door to open it. The photo at left shows the holes with the doors closed, and at right they are open. Note the release buttons next to each hole.

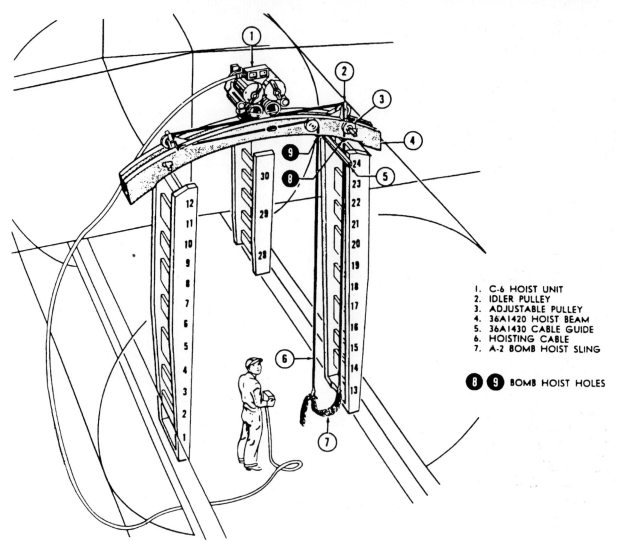

1. C-6 HOIST UNIT
2. IDLER PULLEY
3. ADJUSTABLE PULLEY
4. 36A1420 HOIST BEAM
5. 36A1430 CABLE GUIDE
6. HOISTING CABLE
7. A-2 BOMB HOIST SLING

8 9 BOMB HOIST HOLES

This drawing illustrates the method of loading conventional bombs using the C-6 hoist unit on the top of the aircraft.
(General Dynamics via Moore)

DEFENSIVE ARMAMENT

A close-up photo shows the nose turret with the gun enclosure and dome assembly panel removed.   (USAF)

This nose gun installation is undergoing maintenance at Ellsworth AFB. The guns and their associated equipment were easily accessed so long as the maintenance men were not afraid of heights!   (USAFHRC)

This side view shows the nose gun installation and its hemispheric sight. The nose guns were angled downward, as seen in this view, when they were in the stowed or "at rest" position. Note that the bomb sighting window has been replaced with a solid panel.   This became possible on B-36Ds when a hemispheric bomb sight was added to the underside of the nose. See page 63.   (USAF)

Above left: The initial tail turret and radar configuration is shown on the YB-36. The single small radome housed the antenna for the AN/APG-3 radar system. The AN/APG-32, fitted in the B-36D, utilized the same radome.

(USAF Museum)

Above right: On late B-36F aircraft, a second radar antenna was added to the tail system and a larger fairing was added to the structure directly beneath the rudder. This just doubled the AN/APG-32 system and was known as the AN/APG-32A. This radome configuration was also used by the later AN/APG-41. *(USAF)*

Left: A wide single radome was designed to replace the twin radomes of the AN/APG-41 on later variants. It was also retrofitted to earlier tail numbers. Note the thin metal strips that close the slots in which the guns move vertically. The strips coiled around rollers in the two sliding boxes through which the barrels protruded. The guns have been removed from this aircraft. *(Hayes)*

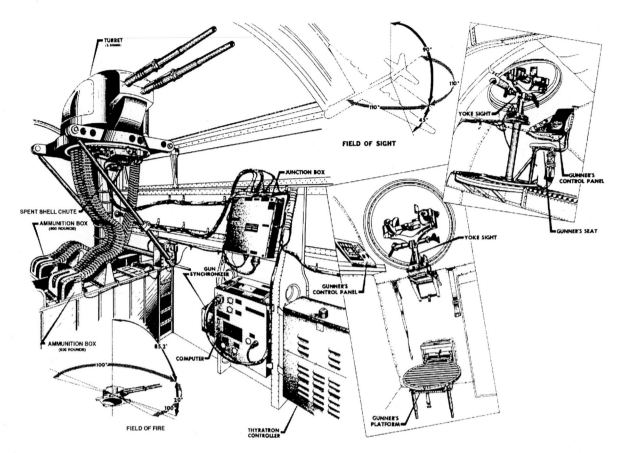

The interior of an upper turret is shown in this drawing. The placement of the equipment is evident, and the other side of the bay was essentially a mirror image of what is shown here. Note the slightly different sight for the upper stations as compared to that shown in the drawing below, and that the forward gunners stood on a small platform instead of having a seat.

(USAF via Cripliver)

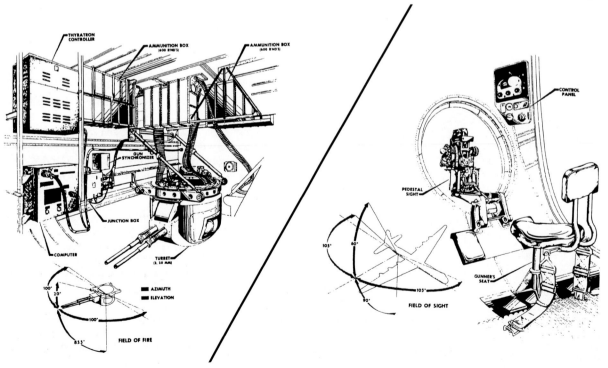

This drawing shows the lower right gun turret and its associated electronics. The lower left gun bay was a mirror image of this. The lower right gunner's station is also shown with the sight in the extended position. The sight pivoted on its base to swing out of the way so that the blister could be used for scanning the engines and flaps.

(USAF via Cripliver)

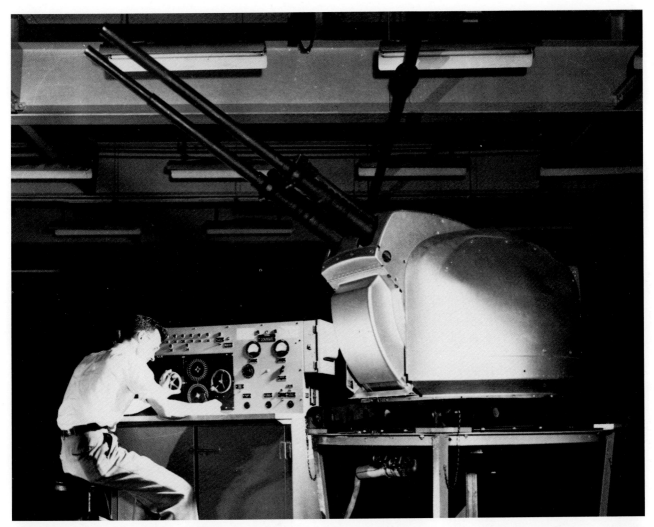

A complete turret undergoes final tests at General Electric's plant before being delivered to the Air Force. (USAF)

At left is a photograph showing the lower aft turret with the side panels removed from the individual guns. Some of the supporting racks and ammunition cans can be seen in the bay. The gunner for the right, upper, aft turret can be seen in the photo at right. His seat and his sight are clearly visible. Note that the sight projects out into the sighting blister and is mounted vertically.

(Both USAFHRC)

ANTENNAS

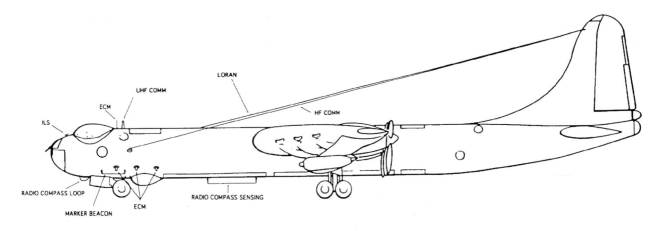

The antenna configuration used on a typical B-36D is shown in this drawing. The ECM antennas were repeated on the right side, but all others shown were a single antenna. The radio compass sensing antenna was mounted just left of centerline on the left bomb bay door.

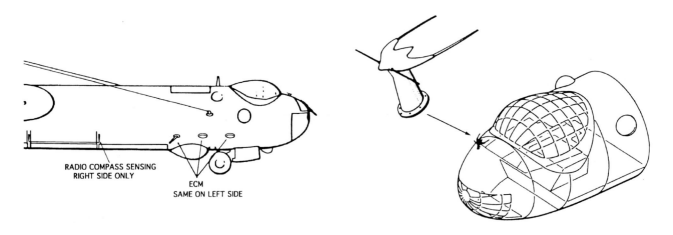

On the B-36B aircraft, the radio compass sensing antenna was mounted on the right side of the fuselage with the masts mounted between the tracks of the sliding bomb bay doors. Small radomes covered the early ECM antennas.

This drawing shows the configuration of the early ILS antenna.

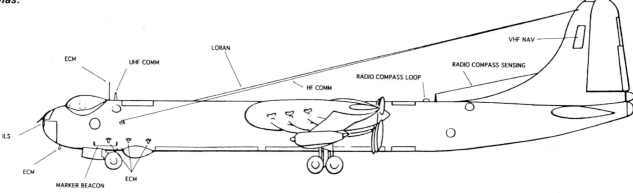

The antenna configuration on B-36F and later aircraft was also retrofitted to some B-36Ds. The ILS antenna was moved to a flush sensor mounted in place of the small circular window pane in the nose glazing. The radio compass sensing and loop antennas were moved to the spine just aft of the rear turret, and several ECM antennas were added. The VHF navigation antenna was a flush dielectric panel on the sides of the vertical tail. Later, the clothesline antenna for the marker beacon was replaced with a circular flush-mounted antenna on the fuselage bottom just aft of the nose gear.

The loop antenna radome and the stub mast for the radio compass sensing antenna can be seen here on the spine of the aircraft. They are located just aft of the rear turret door.

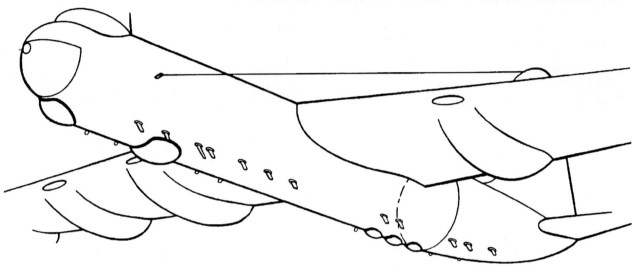

In addition to the normal compliment of communications and navigation antennas, the RB-36s carried a forest of ECM transmitting and sensing antennas. This drawing shows the nominal placement of these antennas, but the configurations could change with equipment and mission. Normally, the ECM antennas were paired from side to side.

This close-up shows one of the ECM antenna mounts. The center plug would be removed and the stub antenna would then be inserted into the resulting hole. The nose of the aircraft is to the right. Note the streamlined airfoil shape of the antenna's cross section.

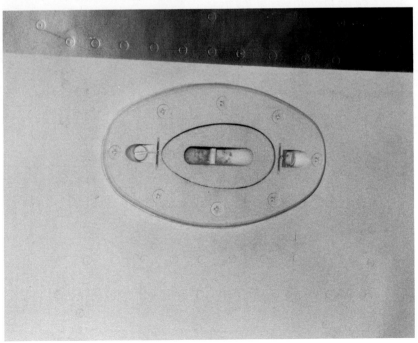

EXTERIOR LIGHTING

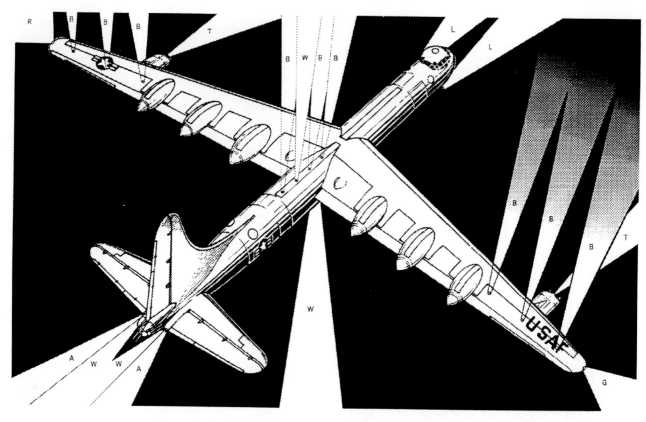

This drawing shows the positions of the multitude of exterior lights fitted on the B-36. The landing and taxi lights are coded L and T respectively. The navigation and position lights are coded with the first letter of their color; R = red, G = green, A = amber, and W = white. The nine formation lights are blue and are coded B. *(USAF)*

This photo shows the landing light and pitot tube on the left side of the nose. The installation on the right side was identical. *(Kinzey)*

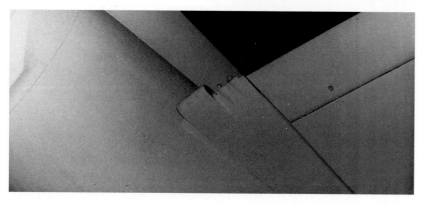

The tail navigation lights were located on the trailing edge of the horizontal stabilizer. The inner light was white, and the other light was amber. The fitting inboard of the lights was the receiving antenna for the AN/APS-54 radar warning system fitted to the aircraft in the mid-1950s. This installation of lights and the antenna is mirrored on the left side of the tail.

MISCELLANEOUS DETAILS

Details of the canopy structure used on all production B-36 variants can be seen in this view. Note the two windshield wipers and the hatch to the right in the photograph. (USAF)

This close-up of the nose section provides a good look and the canopy and nose glazing on a B-36B. Note the windshield wiper on the large circular flat piece in the nose glazing. The circular glass piece was for the bomb aiming device, and it was later replaced with a metal plate after the hemispherical bomb sight became standard. It was located under the nose section as illustrated in the photograph at right. (USAF)

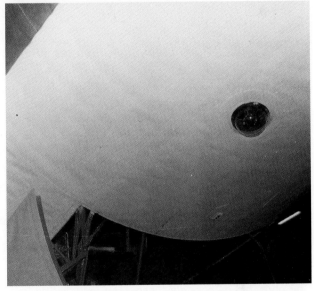

On B-36D and subsequent models, a hemispheric bomb sight replaced the sight using the flat sighting window in the nose glazing. This view is from the right front. It is right of centerline and about four feet forward of the nose gear well.

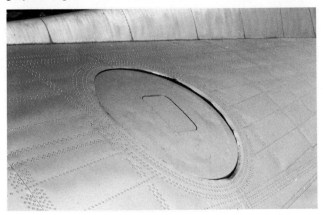

When the aircraft went through the Featherweight programs, some of the sighting blisters were replaced by flat plugs with a small clear panel. In this photo, the clear panel has been painted over. The two lower aft blisters were usually retained for use by scanners. (Hayes)

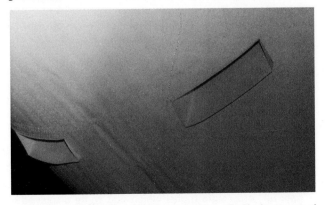

Under the aft fuselage there were two chaff chutes, and these were present on all B-36 variants. They were added during the production run of the B-36F, but they were also retrofitted to earlier aircraft. They are even with the leading edge of the horizontal stabilizer and are indicated on the five-view scale drawings on page 43.

MODELERS SECTION
KIT REVIEWS

The small Aurora kit was in 1/333rd scale, and although it was very small, it came complete with landing gear.

(Kinzey)

1/333rd Scale Kit

Aurora B-36, Kit Number 492

The smallest kit of the B-36 that has been released dates back to 1957, and it was issued by Aurora in the United States and Holland. Although both issues had the same kit number, the box art was different. This tiny model came complete with production landing gear and jet engine pods. A clear stand was also provided, but the only clear parts for the model itself were the canopy and nose glazing. The blisters were represented only by raised scribing in the form of circles on the fuselage.

Forty silver parts represented a rather generic looking B-36, with no particular variant being readily identified. The serial number for the tail was **15720**, which would indicate a B-36H, but the propellers had the rounded tips of the earlier aircraft. A single stub represented the two tail guns, but no nose guns were provided. The doors for the turrets and bomb bays were engraved into the plastic.

In addition to the serial number on the tail, four national insignias for the fuselage and wings, two **USAF** markings for the upper right and lower left wing panels, and two small **UNITED STATES AIR FORCE** markings were provided on the decal sheet. There was also a triangular shaped decal for the stand. Locations for the decals were scribed into the plastic to make sure they were positioned properly.

Today, this kit is considered to be a collector's item, and the U. S. issue brings from ten to fifteen dollars. The release from Holland is valued in the fifteen to twenty dollar range.

1/181st Scale Kit

Revell B-36, Various Kit Numbers

Originally issued in the mid-1950s, this kit was a "gear up" or in-flight model which was to be displayed on Revell's "Revolving" or swiveling stand. This allowed the model to be displayed in various attitudes. Later releases deleted the swiveling stand and replaced it with one of a conventional fixed "tab and slot" design. The first release had a kit number of H205, while H209 was a gift set in which the B-36 was packaged with other Revell bomber

The Revell kit dates back to the 1950s, and it does not accurately represent any specific B-36 variant. It therefore cannot be considered by the serious scale modeler and is best left to the kit collectors. The original box art is at the top in this photo, and the later art used with kit 139 is at the bottom.

(Kinzey)

kits. The same model was released again as a single kit with the number H-139 in the United States, Australia, Brazil, Japan, New Zealand, and Mexico.

A feature found on kits that date back to the 1950s was raised locations for the decals, and these are present on this kit as well. Markings were limited to the national insignia for the wings and fuselage, **USAF** for the upper right and lower left wings, **UNITED STATES AIR FORCE** for the fuselage sides, and insignias for each side of the nose. The serial number (452057) is not correct for any B-36 ever built, but the last four digits would correspond to a block 10 B-36B.

Due to its small size, there is very little in the way of details, and no nose or tail guns are included. The engraved bomb bay doors are the early sliding types used on the B-36A and B-36B, and the upper turret doors have the cutout for the life raft which is only correct for the A and B variants. However, the jet engine pods for the later versions are provided, so take your pick!

Clear parts include a canopy, a nose piece, and small beads that are to be glued into matching depressions to represent sighting blisters.

Because this kit does not accurately represent any version of the B-36, it is not one that can be considered by the serious scale modeler. It therefore only has interest to collectors. The original issue is valued in the thirty to fifty dollar range, while kit H-139 brings only eight to twelve dollars. The gift set is very rare and has a value of two hundred dollars and up.

This Revell kit is in the "ball park" of a 1/144th scale B-36, although it is a little undersized for this scale. However, it is close enough to illustrate that the Peacemaker would make an excellent subject for a quality "state-of-the-art model in 1/144th scale. Hopefully, some model company will soon issue such a model that can go into collections of other large scale military and commercial aircraft.

1/72nd Scale Kits

Sutcliff B-36, No Kit Number

The first kit of the B-36 in 1/72nd scale was a vacuformed release from Contrail that was marketed under the Sutcliff label. It provided only the basic shapes of the parts with no details whatsoever. When the Monogram kit came out, this kit seemed to vanish off the face of the earth. Collectors' catalogs list it as being worth between twenty-five and thirty-five dollars, but there are two problems. The first is to find one of these kits, and the second is to find someone who wants it. Even with the Monogram kit becoming more difficult to find, this vacuformed release cannot be considered by the scale modeler.

Monogram B-36, Kit Numbers 5703 & 5707

When Monogram released this kit in 1980, it was billed as the largest model airplane kit ever produced, and with the exceptions of some large scale vacu-forms, it still is. The kit is molded in gray styrene with raised panel lines and features the crisp clean molding found in most Monogram releases. The clear parts are commendably thin and clear, but the sighting blisters are slightly undersized to fit properly into the holes in the fuselage.

The major problem the model builder will face is that the kit does not accurately represent any B-36 or RB-36 aircraft if it is built straight from the box. It most closely matches the RB-36H in that it has two flight engineer stations on the flight deck, panel lines showing the various camera doors, and the ferret ECM antenna radomes. The problem is that, as built, the kit falls between two separate RB-36 configurations. To help illustrate this problem, drawings have been included with this review. In the drawing of the configuration before T.O. 1B-36(R)-216, it can be seen that the aircraft had ferret ECM antenna radomes mounted on the belly of what was bomb bay 4. A 33' 8" long bomb bay, configured to hold 100-pound photoflash bombs in bay 2, and an auxiliary fuel tank in bay 3 extended from bay 4 to the rear of the camera compartment. This is what Monogram has modeled, although it is a scale 1' 8'' short. Now, compare this to the configuration after T.O. 1B-36(R)-216. This modification was done to give the RB-36s a conventional and nuclear bombing capability, and it moved the ferret ECM gear from bay 4 and relocated it to a position aft of the rear pressure compartment. This left

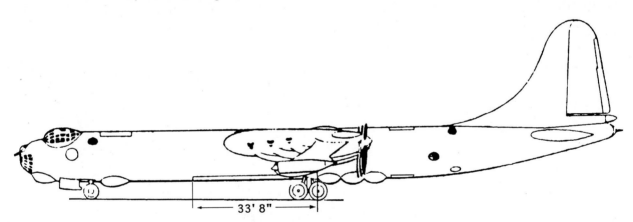

This drawing shows the location of the bomb bay for the photoflash bombs on RB-36 aircraft before T.O. 1B-36(R)-216.   *(USAF)*

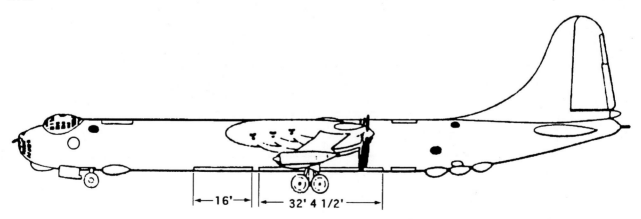

After the implementation of T.O. 1B-36(R)-216, the locations of the weapons bays were as shown in this drawing. This T.O. enabled the RB-36 aircraft to carry conventional and special weapons. Note also the new locations of the aft ECM radomes.
(USAF)

bomb bays 3 and 4 identical to that of the B-36B bombers and there was a short 16-foot bay (bay two) aft of the camera compartment. What the kit has is the single bay before the T.O. change, but the ferret radomes are located on the rear fuselage as on the aircraft after the T.O.

To build the kit without having to get into the modification business, the modeler should built the kit according to the instructions to make an RB-36, but the aft ECM radomes should be placed under bay 4 instead of on the rear fuselage. This will result in a relatively accurate RB-36H. It will limit the number of markings however, because only the 5th, 28th, 72nd, and 99th wings used RB-36s. Further, the T.O., which changed the configuration to allow bombing, appears to have been issued before the white anti-flash paint was added in the 1955-56 time period.

One last item is required to make an accurate RB-36. There were four small windows in the camera compartment, and these are represented on the kit in the form of raised panel lines. They should be cut open, and clear windows should be installed. The aft window on the left side is in the center of an oval escape hatch, so scribe the hatch to make it look as though it is removable. The 100-pound photoflash bombs included with the kit should be painted gray according to a period tech order, however no Federal Standard number for the gray was provided.

To build an accurate bomber version from the kit will take some extra conversion work, and more time and effort will be required to correct some of the errors that

Monogram made. In describing what needs to be done, this review will begin at the nose and work aft toward the tail.

The nose and its related clear parts will do very well as molded, but there are some things that can be improved. Since the nose guns are included, a featherweight aircraft cannot be modeled without removing parts 56 and 57, then fairing over this area. On late B-36Ds and subsequent versions, the ILS antenna was changed from the external type mounted forward of the windshield to a flush-mounted antenna in place of the small circular window in the clear lower nose piece (part 96). The solution is to paint the small window flat black on these later versions.

The bases for the pitot tubes have been molded on each side of the nose, but no pitot tubes are included or mentioned in the instructions. These must be made from scrap plastic and added using the photographs in this book for reference. The landing lights are molded just below and aft of the pitots, but they will look much better if they are replaced with MV lenses.

If an earlier variant than the B-36H is desired, the extra flight engineer's station should be removed, and to be completely correct, the configuration of the engineer's panel should be changed. This is also the time to add weight to the nose area in order to avoid having to use a tail support on the finished model. It will take a lot of weight, but there is plenty of room to hide it in. The interior of the large radome is a dandy spot for a slug of

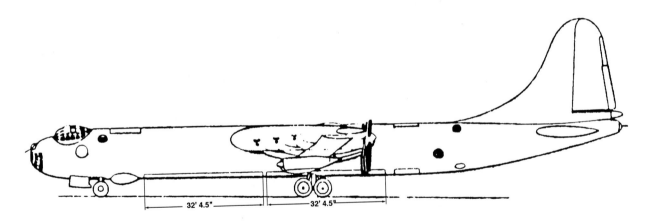

The standard bomb bay configuration for B-36 bomber variants is shown in this drawing.   (USAF)

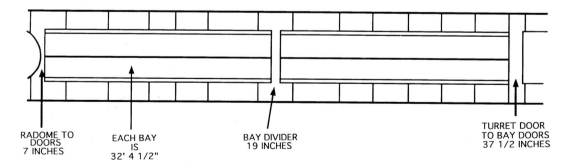

This drawing provides the key dimensions for modelers who want to represent the standard bomb bay configuration for B-36 bomber variants on the Monogram kit. Actual dimensions are provided and should be divided by 72 to get scale dimensions.

Walthers TEMPLOW.

Aft of the large radome, the recessed location for the Trimetrogon cameras (parts 18) must be filled in along with the two door tracks. Using the drawings in this book as a guide, remove the panel lines for the camera windows as well as the windows and hatch for the camera compartment. When cleaning up the fuselage join line, remember the forward turret doors split on the centerline and retract to each side. However, the aft turrets were covered by single piece doors.

The easy way to fix the bomb bay is to attach the doors in the closed position. Then fill all the seams and accurately rescribe the doors. If the doors are placed in the open position, the interior detailing in the bomb bay must be extended by scratchbuilding, and a new set of doors must be constructed using photographs in this book for reference. All photographs that show the doors open on the ground show both sets open, so there is a tremendous amount of detailing to do, especially if the universal racks are to be included. For those wishing to add the ultimate in detail, the bomb hoist holes may be scribed into the skin on top of the bays using the template provided in this review.

Photographs of the bombers show the external ECM antennas only in the first three locations on the fuselage sides, so the sockets for the other eight should be removed. The small radome on the fuselage top, which is located just aft of the upper turret doors, is where the loop antenna was placed when it was moved from the chin position. This happened on the B-36F and later versions, so if one of these aircraft is being modeled, retain the small radome and construct the short post and wire antenna for the radio compass again using the drawings and photographs in this book for reference. If backdating to an earlier model is necessary, remove the radome and construct the small chin unit along with the short clothesline antenna just above the left nose gear door.

The hard part concerns the tail gun and radar. What comes in the kit is correct for the later B-36F, H, and J versions. But this will have to be changed if most of the decals on the market are to be used. The large radome fairing will have to be removed and the hole filled with scrap plastic and filler to leave a flat surface where a new smaller fairing can be attached. The new fairing can be scratchbuilt using a spare drop tank from another kit. If a late variant is being modeled, the large fairing may be left as is, but try to find photographs of the actual aircraft being modeled to determine if the late single-piece radome is appropriate. Such a cover may be vacu-formed over a mold made from the two kit radomes and some filler.

If a B-36A or B version is desired, then a tail bumper must be added, and the tracks for the sliding bomb bay doors must be made from scratch. These tracks looked like those for the turret doors, and their correct locations can be determined from the photographs in this book. References, in the form of photographs and drawings, are likewise included to show the correct locations and configurations of the various communications and ECM antennas, so read through the book carefully before you begin. Early aircraft (prior to 44-92098) also had a different spoke pattern on the main gear wheels that must be duplicated if accuracy is to be maintained.

For the truly dedicated builder, there are four square holes near the tip of the vertical tail which were exhausts for the anti-icing air. Monogram included these on the undersides of the horizontal tail, but missed the ones on the tip of the fin. Using those on the underside of the horizontal tail as a pattern for size, add a set on each side of the vertical tail.

As can be seen in the photographs, the tail guns did not move up and down in open slots, so use some tape or five-thousandths sheet plastic to close these holes for a more realistic look.

As mentioned earlier, the sighting blisters included in the kit are marginally too small, however they make excellent masters that can be used to vacu-form new ones. Add a disk of forty-thousandths styrene to the base

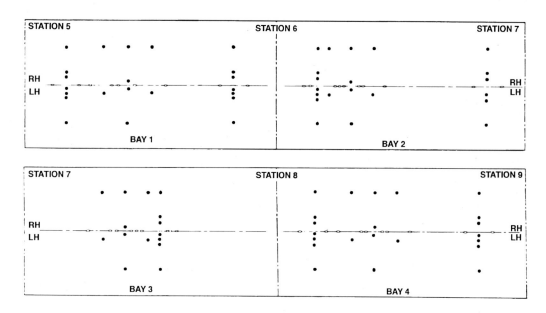

This drawing shows the location of the bomb hoist holes on the top of the fuselage. It is reproduced in 1/72nd scale and may be used as a template for modelers wishing to duplicate this feature.

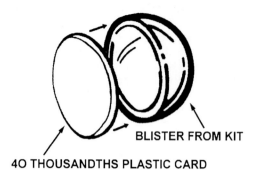

BLISTER FROM KIT

40 THOUSANDTHS PLASTIC CARD

This drawing illustrates the method of attaching a disc of plastic to the base of the sighting blisters prior to using them as molds for vacu-forming new blisters which will fit better than those supplied in the kit.

of a kit-supplied blister as shown in the accompanying drawing to make a master. After vacu-forming a new set of blisters, they will be a snap fit in the sighting positions.

The wings will not require a lot of work, and there was little change to them between variants. The location of the bullet sealing pads under the center and outer wing fuel tanks is indicated on the model. To be completely accurate for a non-featherweight aircraft, these pads should be added using tape for the pads themselves, and strips of decals for the fairing strips at the edges of the pads. The locations of the blue formation lights are marked on the wings, but not on the fuselage. Some lenses need to be added here.

Obviously, if a model of an aircraft without jet engines is to be built, the mounting holes in the wings must be filled in, and the missing details under where the pylons would go must be scribed into place. The kit propellers have the square tips, but it is simple to round off the tips for an early aircraft if care is taken to insure constant prop diameter throughout.

There was a taxi light under the jet intakes, and

Monogram left it off. This can be duplicated easily by cutting a small notch into the fairing then filling it with Kristal Kleer. A more ambitious solution would be to make a small lens from clear plastic. Refer to the top photograph on page 52 for reference.

Perhaps more difficult, and maybe not worth the effort for most modelers, are the air plugs at the rear of each engine cowling. The kit has been molded with the cowling slightly too long, so the absence of the air plugs is not noticeable. This means that if the plugs are to be duplicated, the cowlings will have to be shortened. Having done that, a piece of thin tubing the correct diameter and length may be fastened in the cowling to simulate the air plug. But in order to do this, the props must be left off until the plugs are added. This is a good idea in any event, because they are definitely in the way when finishing the aircraft. Further, the seam between the prop and the rear part of the spinner is a major problem to fix after the props are installed. To remedy this, carefully remove enough plastic from part 37 to allow it to slip into the engine cowling after the wing top and bottom have been assembled. (Do the fitting with the wing halves taped together.) Then carefully remove enough of the rear face of the sockets in the cowlings to allow part 37 to be inserted from the rear as shown in the drawing. The goal is to make this part a snap fit, and with some care this can be accomplished. Then the props can be finished as units and inserted with a drop of glue as the last step after all finishing is accomplished. Another point that should be made is that the propellers on the non-featherweight aircraft had exhausts for the prop anti-icing air on the forward part of the spinner.

The fleet was bare metal until the 1955-56 time period when the anti-flash white paint was applied to the undersides. At the same time, protective clear and aluminized acrylic paint was applied to the rest of the aircraft. This paint tended to weather, thus leaving some of the Peacemakers with a decidedly unkept look until repainting could be accomplished.

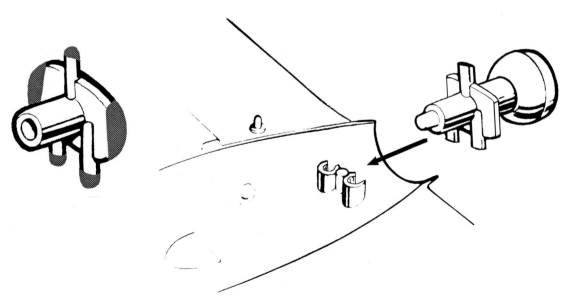

The shaded areas to be removed from all parts 37 are shown here. This will allow the propellers to be installed later after finishing is complete.

This model was built by the author and was backdated to the B-36D configuration by modifying the props, rescribing the bomb bay doors, and rebuilding the radome for the tail gun radar and its fairing.

This model was built by Al Lloyd, and it duplicates the heavy weathering that was common on aircraft after they were painted silver on the sides and upper surfaces and anti-thermal white on the undersides.　　　*(Lloyd)*

The decal sheet that came with the original issue of Monogram's B-36 (kit number 5703) had markings for two aircraft. The first was B-36H, 01087, which was from the 42nd Bomb Wing, and the second was an RB-36H with no unit markings. The sheet was very rudimentary with only the cockpit instrument panels, basic Air Force markings, national insignia, and SAC's star spangled band. The 42nd Wing insignia, SAC's crest, and a red band were provided as tail markings. Given the rather plain schemes of the late model B-36s with the white anti-thermal paint, this is not a bad sheet, however the adhesion of the decals is not as good as might be expected.

For the second release of this model (kit number 5707) an entirely new sheet was included, and it is of very high quality. In addition to the basic Air Force markings and national insignia, it again has the cockpit instrument panels. Additionally, the propeller markings are included along with the common smoking prohibition warning seen on the nose wheel doors.

One set of markings is for a B-36D of the 7th Bomb Wing of the 8th Air Force, and it has Triangle J tail markings. A second set of markings is for an RB-36E of the 5th Strategic Recon Wing with Circle X tail markings. The decal sheet is excellent with sharp definition and accurate registration.

The problem with this sheet results from poor research on Monogram's part. Neither a B-36D or an RB-36E, as represented on the decal sheet, can be built from the kit as it comes in the box. In order to use the markings on this sheet, the modeler will have to do some conversion work. Both the B-36D and the RB-36E had the single radome with the small fairing for the tail gun radar instead of the dual radar set with the large fairing that comes in the kit. So the large fairing for the tail radar must be cut away and plastic card and filler must be used to construct the earlier smaller fairing. Then, to be completely accurate, the spoke pattern for the main gear wheels must be corrected to represent the early type which appeared on the B-36A, B, E, and those Ds that were remanufactured from Bs. The instructions show these aircraft to be bare metal which is correct for the period when the large geometric designs were used on the tail.

In spite of the problems discussed in this review, this kit still rates as an excellent model, and it is probably the only one serious scale modelers will ever have to work with in building a B-36. By spending the required time to correct and convert as necessary, an excellent model will result. It can also be used as a basis for building conversions of the XC-99 and YB-60 aircraft. The sheer size alone of these models in 1/72nd scale would be very impressive indeed!

The Monogram B-36 kit was the basis for this conversion to the XC-99 by Mark Young. *(Young)*

Mark Young also used the Monogram B-36 as the basis for this conversion to the YB-60. *(Young)*

AFTER-MARKET DECALS

Note: Because there are so few after-market decals available for the B-36, all of which are for the Monogram kit in 1/72nd scale, we are able to give more information than usual for these few sheets.

Scalemaster Sheet Number SM-28

The first of two sheets from Scalemaster for the Monogram 1/72nd scale B-36 features markings for a B-36D from the 92nd Bomb Wing. It has the wing insignia for the left side of the nose and squadron insignias for three different squadrons for the right side. Also included are the Circle W markings and serial numbers for the tail. National markings must be taken from kit decals or other after-market sheets. The decals are thin, adhere well, and the register is excellent. The difficulty lies in the fact that these markings are for an aircraft that cannot be built out-of-the box from the Monogram kit. The modeler must modify the tail radome from the large dual fairing to the small single radome for the tail gun radar. Further, the spoke pattern for the main gear wheels must be corrected to the early type used on the B-36Ds that were remanufactured from B-36Bs.

Scalemaster Sheet Number SM-31

The second sheet from Scalemaster for the B-36 provides markings for a B-36H from the 11th Bomb Wing. It includes wing insignia for both sides of the nose, aircraft tail and buzz numbers, markings for the propellers, 8th Air Force markings, and red and white markings for the jet pods. The large Triangle U markings for the 11th BW are also on the sheet along with decals for the nose wheel doors. These show the tail number on a red and white striped background. This sheet will be correct on the kit as built from the box, because the kit accurately represents the physical configuration of the B-36H. Photos of this aircraft show that it had a squadron insignia on the right side of the nose and the wing insignia on the left side, instead of having the wing insignia on both sides. This illustrates the dangers of developing a decal sheet with references for only one side of the subject. With that error in mind however, this is the only after-market sheet that can be used on the Monogram kit as it comes in the box.

SuperScale Sheet Number 72-271

The first sheet from SuperScale (formerly Microscale) for Monogram's 1/72nd scale B-36 includes markings for a B-36A and a B-36B from the 7th Bomb Wing at Carswell Air Force Base. Tail numbers, large buzz numbers, the 8th Air Force insignia, three 7th Bomb Wing insignias, and **NO SMOKING** warnings for the nose wheel doors are all provided. Black stripes to make the large triangle for the vertical tail are also supplied.

Although the graphics on the instruction sheet are correct, the drawings are misidentified. The model numbers are reversed so that the tail number for the B-36B is shown for the B-36A.

The decals are up to the usual quality expected from SuperScale, and the modeler should have no problem using them. With the red high-visibility markings on the tail and wings, the B-36B would make a striking model.

The major problem is that there is no kit of a B-36A or a B-36B on the market, so it will take more than just

leaving the jet pods off of the Monogram kit in order to build either of these early variants. Aside form the modifications listed elsewhere in this book that are required to backdate the kit to a B-36D or B-36E, the B-36A and B-36B variants had four sets of sliding bomb bay doors and a retractable tail bumper. Additionally, they used props with round tips, so there is some heavy duty conversion work ahead for anyone wanting to use this decal sheet on an accurate model.

SuperScale Sheet Number 72-272

Markings for two aircraft are provided on this sheet. The first is an RB-36F from the 99th Strategic Reconnaissance Wing, and it has the star spangled band with the SAC insignia for both sides of the nose. Large **U. S. AIR FORCE** markings and buzz numbers for the fuselage sides are likewise included. The red and white checkered fin tip and nose wheel door markings are provided along with some walkway and **NO STEP** decals.

The instruction sheet shows the aircraft with the white anti-thermal paint on the undersides, and this was correct for the later life of this particular aircraft. In the pre-1956 time frame, the same aircraft would be correct in a bare metal scheme without the anti-thermal paint. Unfortunately, this aircraft was the first RB-36F built, and photographs of it in 1956 show it to have the small APG-32 tail radar. This means that the Monogram kit must be back-dated with the small radome fairing to be correct.

The second aircraft on this sheet is RB-36H, 52-1382, from the 7th Bomb Wing. The aircraft is identified on the instruction sheet as a B-36H, and the scheme is shown in an earlier publication on the Peacemaker as a B-36. However, the tail number clearly identifies the aircraft as an RB-36H, and the 7th BW is not known to have had any RB-36s assigned. It is suggested that the modeler use a different serial number that is correct for a bomber and leave the decal for the blue fin tip off unless photographic evidence can be found to substantiate that this scheme is accurate for an RB-36.

Markings for this aircraft include the star spangled band with the 7th BW insignia, **U. S. AIR FORCE** markings for the fuselage sides, and the contentious "last three" of the tail number for the fuselage sides. The blue fin cap decal is also included, but its use is also suspect in light of the erroneous model identification. As with other Super-Scale sheets, the national insignia and other generic markings must be taken from the kit decals or other after-market sheets.

SUMMARY

The modeler is left with the original kit decals (from kit number 5703) and Scalemaster's sheet number SM-31 as sources for decals that can be correctly applied to a model built straight from the box. All other schemes require at least some modification to the kit, and in a few cases, extensive conversion work is necessary.